LEARN A MAN

EARN A MAN

Sharp advice for women

"Get him… keep him"
Learn his heart, earn his commitment,
The mysteries of how men think,
whether
Husband, Lover or Friend with benefits.

by

Barry Fletcher

We at Barry Fletcher Products hope you enjoy this book, a product that connects truth with your real needs and challenges. This book was not written as a tutorial or guidebook. The views expressed are the opinions of the author.

Published by Barry Fletcher Products
6304 Marlboro Pike
District Heights, MD 20747

Visit our website for more information:
www.barryfletcher.com

All photographs are used by permission.

First edition.

ISBN: 9781-61658-270-8
Library of Congress Control Number: 2010905899

Also by Barry Fletcher

Why Are Black Women Losing Their Hair?

Hair is Sexual

CONTENTS

Foreword
By Donnie Simpson
Radio and TV Host

Throughout his illustrious, ever-changing career in cosmetology, Barry Fletcher's ideas and techniques have had a major impact on the way we look at beauty and hair fashions. Next to Vidal Sassoon and Paul Mitchell, he has trained and influenced more hairdressers than anyone in the industry. Barry could have rested on his laurels years ago, after winning a Rolls-Royce in 1985 or becoming the first African American to win a position on the U.S. Hair Olympics Team with a black model in 1994. His work could be seen on countless celebrities and magazine covers. He started his own hair care product line in 1992, wrote the book *Why Are Black Women Losing Their Hair?* in 2000 and *Hair is Sexual* in 2003. Fletch, as many of his friends call him, is a true visionary. He is always in front of the wave and on the beach chillin' by the time the tide brings everyone else in. I have always found Barry to be very inspirational and I'm honored that he wanted me to be a part of his vision by writing this foreword.

Barry is an ardent bachelor, so my wife won't allow me to hang with him much, but I have always felt that he had a keen eye for life and compelling conversation for the ladies in particular. We have been friends since 1987 when he first cut my hair and I noticed his enthusiastic awareness of his social environment. He spoke about relationships with a certain knowledge and confidence that can only come from experience. He never was one for perpetrating or pretending and stayed true to his beliefs for socially coexisting. It's not surprising that he decided to take on the hefty task of clarifying men's thoughts about relationships.

After 30 years of working with men and women in the community, he has become an incredibly popular and influential personality. Fasten your seat belt, and prepare for an emotional roller-coaster ride. I'm sure you'll find this book enlightening, truthful, disturbing, poetic and entertaining. Barry Fletcher is about to let you get out in front of the wave too. Hold on, surf's up.

Acknowledgments

Gye-Nyame Na Obeye...Only God can do it! I thank Him for blessing me with two wonderful parents who formed and shaped the man I am today. May they rest in peace.

I would like to acknowledge and express my gratitude to those who contributed to my journey and the creation of this book:

- My family, friends and clients for their agape love and support,

- Donnie Simpson for his gracious *Foreword*,

- Jon Perkins and Amy Alexander, my editors,

- Marcille Moss for helping me in so many ways... I will always remember,

- Big sis Gloria Jean Jackson for her tireless proofing,

- K. Michael Jordan for his help with *Boys to Men*, and Anthony Nutt and Kenn Blanchard for their help with *If Jesus Were One of Us*,

- Floyd Kenyatta, my consultant,

- LaShawn Hackley, Marie Little and Concha Johnson for proofing,

- Damond Andrews for the cover design,

- Andras Spiegel for the book design,

- Margarita Sweet, Quincy Richardson, Robin Murphy, Doreen Price, Joycelyn Bacchus, Sharon Smith, Dr. Monica Crawford Roberts, Liana Robinson, Michelle Shackaford, Otelia Simon, Gregory Jones, Tonya Cook, Brigetta Weatherington, Lelia Pray and Marcus Gray for their feedback,

- Legend models: Eniola Eboda, Gavin Webb, Moses Mario Sourec, Mel Jones and Karl Jones. Models: Bill Madison, Francis Stewart, Gregory Quadebaum, David Somerville, Dennis Schoonmaker, Matt Butler, Rabon Hutcherson II, Antwan Monroe, Stephen Hinton, and Jovite Nguembou.

- Miracles Photography Studio

Special thanks to the wonderful staff at *Barry Fletcher Products* and *The Hair Palace Salon*.

Please extend your prayers and blessings to master hair designer Larry Massenburg as he recovers from surgery.

I am forever grateful!

Back cover autographs (clockwise from top left): Halle Berry, Tina Turner, Dr. Maya Angelou, Senator Carol Moseley-Braun, Donnie Simpson, Chaka Khan, Miki Howard, Super Model Iman, Mary J. Blige, Sheryl Lee Ralph, Eartha Kitt and Patti LaBelle (center)

Preface

I'm tired of men bragging about how they've lied, tricked or misled their wife or girlfriend into thinking they have a happy relationship, while secretly fearing what would happen if the whole truth were to be revealed. You may not like everything a man does, you may not always like the way he makes you feel and you may not like everything I say, but I'm here to give you the truth as I know it. I've gained insight into how men think and their triumphant efforts to please, pleasure and prosper with a woman. It's not always pretty. Ladies, it's time for you to develop a strategy for approaching relationships: mind over emotion. When your emotions get ahead of your reasoning, you become vulnerable to the very hurt you seek to avoid. Can we talk honestly?

When a man makes you feel more like the lady you aspire to become, that's probably a good time to consider investing in his potential. As you're attempting to judge his character, how do you discover his virtues? Times are changing and you may need to change your approach, rather than settling for the incompatible men who approach you.

Since 1940 women have outnumbered men in the United States and there's no telling what kinds of insecurities men are dealing with these days. It's going to take a little effort from you. I must admit that I have my own trepidations about marriage and commitment. My ears bleed a lot from other people's stories and since I'm constantly under pressure for answers, I decided to do some more formal research (of the subject) and development (of myself). Read on and learn from my discoveries.

1

Introducing Ladies to Manhood

Every real man needs a woman, but what
he doesn't want you to know... can hurt you

Ladies, forget what you may have read or heard from your mom, your sisters, or your girlfriends. There is a surefire way to *earn a man*. If you sincerely want a man who is worthy of your special light and future promise, a man who can treasure you when you are down as well as he can when you are at the mountaintop, please come right in and pull up a chair. You can take control of how you go about finding him, wooing him and keeping him. You have the power to create an internal and external environment to ensure victory. You can earn a man, not by losing yourself, but by finding yourself.

I am heterosexual man, experienced in the fine arts of loving women, grooming women, and advising women. As a men's barber, I also happen to regularly get an earful of the innermost feelings and thoughts of men who confide in me. Thus, I am in the extremely rare position of hearing both sides – the good, the bad and the boring – from men and from women. At this point, I believe that men who are blessed with the wherewithal to engage in romance – meaning they are not incarcerated, they have a job, are probably educated, and care enough about themselves to come to my shops for regular shape-ups – have a built-in advantage. They are outnumbered by the higher percentage of women who are seeking eligible men. This imbalance creates a certain degree of unfairness for women, and gives men an advantage in the delicate dance of courtship. This is why I am here to provide you with a unique, secret perspective. For those of you who are new at this, or who think they have been there, done that, and bought the T-shirt, or who think that the man's job is to *earn you* while you sit back, Barry Fletcher is here to drop some valuable new information into your romantic toolkit. (And for the sisters who want to hang back, and "make a man prove himself," well, you just haven't had your heart broken enough times, yet.) My sincere wish is that you will hear me *and* listen to me *before* your heart gets shattered into bits and pieces.

The advice and experience I offer here are barometers to help you measure and, if needed, even out your temperament to efficiently find a partner who is your equal. This book will help you neutralize – not hide or bury – your emotions about men, and better assist you as you navigate your search. In the end, if you have read this with an open mind and heart, you will walk away with a clearer understanding and packed arsenal of best practices for finding and winning the man you deserve. Ladies, I know that men often get blamed when relationships go bad, and much of the time that blame is justified. But sometimes women must be willing to look hard at their own behavior, expectations and beliefs. It is not always fair or productive for ladies to automatically blame a man and fail to credit him for his positive aspects, while failing to address their own personal missteps. (All said with love, ladies, only love.)

Now for those of you asking what more is there to learn about men, let me put it to you this way: you will probably not be successful if your goal is to fix or change a man. But by all means, read on if you are interested in learning how to discover effective ways to own and leverage your power, and to use your natural properties to control – er, or should I say, earn a man. **I'm on your side.** This book is written to help empower you. My goal here is to guide you on the path to the man you deserve: someone who is kind, strong, compassionate, tough in all the right ways – and totally, absolutely, one hundred thousand percent SPRUNG on you. My goal is to help you see that you are in control of how much time and access you give a man. Every real man needs a lady, even if he does not know it. Let the lessons begin!

Right now, you might be thinking, "Who is Barry Fletcher, and how is he qualified to give me lessons on how to learn and earn a man?" After thirty years of establishing customer relationships with ladies (through my hair salon) and with brothers (through my barbershop) I have accomplished my goals of becoming a Master Hair Designer and successful entrepreneur who competes in every major hair competition worldwide. My achievements include winning gold medals at major hair design competitions around the globe, a Rolls-Royce automobile and a spot on the USA Hair Olympics team competing in London against teams from 35 countries. I am well traveled and have an established clientele that spans all races and economic levels the world over, from next-door neighbors and stay-at-home moms to career professionals, actresses, politicians, athletes and musicians, including a few names that may be familiar to you: Halle Berry, Sugar Ray Leonard, Prince, Bebe Winans, Iman, Toni Braxton, Senator Carol Mosely-Braun, Tina Turner, Mary J. Blige and Dr. Maya Angelou.

I am an image-maker, a trichologist and an expert in helping clients find the styles that work best for them; a businessman-inventor too, creator of Barry Fletcher Hair Care Products and an expert hair care consultant to Essence Magazine. Throughout my three decades of experience working with clients to improve their hair and personal image, I've developed the skills of a marriage *counselor*, psychologist, therapist, guidance counselor, good listener and social worker. Yes, ladies, I have heard it all.

I have authored two books: my best-selling *Why Are Black Women Losing Their Hair?* and *Hair is Sexual.* But more importantly, I have become a confidant to women who are dealing with their most popular public body part, the one that affects their psyche and confidence the most, the body part that announces them to the rest of the world: their hair. I have a perfect career: working around and for beautiful women. It is a beautiful thing. I love my work, and it shows. The confidence and knowledge I convey with each visit lets ladies know they can rely on me to help them achieve their style and beauty goals. How do we accomplish this? (I say "we" because I am an expert, but not a dictator. I encourage my clients to stay involved, especially if I am totally remaking their look.) I begin by assessing a woman the moment she walks into my hair salon. I realize her beauty needs are immediate, and that I must be accurate.

I cannot write her a prescription, suggesting she "take two a day and get some rest" like some doctors have the luxury of doing. I have a totally different focus when checking out the ladies. *Everything counts!* Her fashion, her demeanor, how she uses her facial muscles and features, her posture and her mannerisms all provide important clues about the general state of her self-esteem. From there, we talk about her desired hair style, which gives me more important clues about her level of vanity and how she perceives her social status. Throughout this part of the process, I am making silent judgments about what I think needs to happen to improve her look, apart from what *she says* she wants, but I do not judge *her.*

You may have heard the old saying that hair stylists are the psychologists of the community. I have learned valuable skills that help with the way I relate to my clients. We all know that if we do not like the way we relate to one another, there can never be a friendship. And we also know that friendship is another, more developed form of *relating.* Good *relations* happen when we start doing things together or for each other. After the two of you confirm that there's good reason to keep it up, it turns into a *relationship*. Yet before that ship sails, you want to make sure you have secured your interest and are strong about your beliefs and values. This is true for women starting new friendships with women and it is most certainly true for women on the verge of relations with a man. We men know that there are goodies on the ship. To us, the goodies are like donuts... glazed donuts, to be squeezed for freshness, licked for sweetness, chewed eagerly, for pure unadulterated pleasure. But here is a small secret about men and their donuts, in case you don't know it already. The only thing better than a glazed donut is a newer, fresher glazed donut. Fiddle-diddle it has a hole in the middle. What I am saying here, with this hole-in-the-middle metaphor is that friends can cum and go, sex is in and out, up and down, but ladies must understand that only true blue relationships last. Before you ever get to that Big Donut of a marriage, you best believe you want your relationship to be on the smoothest seas possible.

So it is that I am confident in my ability to share with you quite a bit about relationships; moreover, to pull back the curtain and let you in on how a man truly thinks. We live in a new day, which requires new strategies to achieve a life filled with love. I subscribe to a theory that is quoted by Oprah Winfrey: "I believe that you are here to become more of yourself and live your best life." Parents, please toss away all the old fairy tale books and the mentality that goes with it. Your daughter will never be Cinderella and neither will your son become Prince Charming. Gone are the days when the number one goal of a young lady was to get married and have 2.3 children. Parents are encouraging their daughters to complete their education, and to wrap themselves around a career and become self-sufficient. A woman's future may have her taking care of the same clueless young man she aspired to marry. We have already seen what happens when a man leaves his family and the woman doesn't have anything to fall back on. Too often, I hear grandmothers talking about how they take care of their grown daughters and their grandchildren, a far cry, I am sure, from what they imagined they would be doing back when they were young ladies.

The latest data show just how "outnumbered" men are and supports my experience-based understanding of why men too often succeed at "playing" women. For men, career choices have become more difficult and sex has become easier. The man knows he can enjoy good sex without marriage. The number of married men in the U.S. has decreased dramatically since the 1960s. According to the U.S. Census Bureau's data on marital status for years 2005-2007, the percentage of men who never married was:

Black	46 percent
Hispanic/Latino	37 percent
Indian	37 percent
Asian	29 percent
White	27 percent

Meanwhile, government data show that roughly 70 percent of black women are single. Ladies, this is what is called a major imbalance.

This book was written to help women spot pivotal points for a lasting relationship. It was written to help you hear and heed that occasional internal alarm that sometimes goes off about some men. Whether you decide to shack or throw him back, take it from date to soul mate, this book will be your trusted guide. I intend to unveil the man's psyche.

This is the book men don't want you to read. At the same time, I will not totally and completely give it all up about my brothers. I cannot, for instance, tell you all the things they say about you, since I believe in accentuating the positive. But in general language and terms, yes... they have called you everything from a queen to a witch. And if the brothers find out I am telling you any of this, they will most definitely call me a snitch!

Yet, in full seriousness, a baseline measurement of a man usually starts on the outside. You take into account his career or job, and the way he works his job; his accomplishments and the amount of money he makes; his education, religion (or lack thereof); and his relationships. I would say it is up to each individual woman to decide how important these measures are in determining his value. However, I suggest that the best way to form a truly useful measuring scale is to place the emphasis on his internal substantive factors. These include how he treats other people, whether he is self-confident, and whether he is patient. And there are his personal traits, which are real and more lasting than superficial items such as what kind of car he drives and how much money he spends on you at a restaurant or in the club.

Our feelings can fluctuate from time to time, but they also represent the core of who we really are: outgoing, guarded, trusting, happy, sad, ambitious, emotional, considerate, strong, weak, etc. Our feelings are connected to our hearts, and to our souls. I would trust a woman with a good heart over a woman with lots of success, money or strong religious values. I've learned to trust the heart, not to say that the heart is an easy place to explore, only that it is the nucleus of all living souls. I've grown comfortable dancing to the heartbeat of the soul. You want a man for the journey, not just for the moment, but the truth is that it's hard, if not impossible, to choose the best life partner if you don't know yourself or what you believe.

Men are tactile, visual, visceral, linear thinking sleuth-hounds. Deep inside every real man is a hero, a "knight in shining armor" who wants to serve and protect his family and loved ones. We are born hunters; our tit-glancing, navel-gazing, ass-watching culture keeps us in constant conflict with some of our hyper-vigilant, under-confident counterparts, women who are overly concerned about our loyalty. It's just second nature for a man to look at the opposite sex... usually it is just a peek! He loves Ms. Right but may lust over Ms. Right-Now. Ladies must be confident enough in themselves and in their relationship with a man not to hassle him if, or when, his eye wanders a bit. You ladies can have it all: a man who is top-ranked, has money in the bank and able to put a *TIGER* in your tank.

A man's senses – what he sees, smells, hears and feels – always trump his sensibilities, which is what your Mama probably called good sense. Remember this: the most fundamental need a man has in a relationship is to feel important and respected for who he is. A man needs financial security; a woman needs emotional security, closeness, and financial security. Men think in straight lines; too many details at one time frustrate us. We want information that is actionable vs. emotional. Oftentimes it is in the best interest of women to work through their emotions separately and then to discuss with their man what needs to happen to remedy the situation. The nonverbal aspects of communication make up 92 percent of a message, while only 8 percent of the impact is verbal. If we can't fix your problem, we don't want to hear about it.

Here is another reason why men tend to have less trouble with relationships than women. If we like what our senses are telling us about you, we'll accept what is offered in the relation and get the rest of the things we need elsewhere, in the interest of preservation. We are not trying to change you ladies and we don't get upset about your lack of interest in, say, sports for example. I cringe when I see a man moping around a department store bored stiff while his lady goes shopping. Ladies, do you really think your man wants to be there holding your purse while you try on another outfit, or another shoe? Would you be okay with it if he insisted that you hang with him when he goes to buy a new golf club, or shoot hoops with his boys on the weekends? Right. So if you think his silence means that he is okay with it, think again. That silence may just mean that he is thinking about how he never asks *you* to engage in *his* down time, or manly pursuits. In that same silence, he may also be starting to resent you for insisting that he go on along to your lady doings. Pick your battles, ladies. Learn to give your man his space, lest he feel confined.

I hear some women sound so wounded, upset and frustrated with men who won't commit to them. Now let's get to the root of this prevailing complexity between men and women. What is commitment anyway? Oftentimes, men think they are committed after the first date; this is the time we start caring, offering kind gestures, becoming more thoughtful and protective. Although this may make us *commitment-worthy*, it only heightens her need for more linguistic persuasions. This is what ladies want to hear come out of a man's mouth: *I want a committed relationship with you, I'm falling in love with you, I want to be with you for the rest of my life and ultimately, will you marry me?* She wants to hear it, have it reinforced and hear it again. To which I say... say it ain't so, ladies! This is the kind of language that turns too many men into liars. He knows, because you either tell him or show him, that you want to hear that. So even if he is not there yet, he soon finds himself saying words that just end up making the lady feel secure, protected and more trusting – falsely. And the irony of this is that it defeats the result that men are actually most concerned with: gaining your trust! Men want to be trusted no matter whether they are worthy or not. Ladies, if you get caught sneaking around checking behind your man, he's going to be very upset upon his discovery. It may be safer for you to warn him before you start snooping. This is the way I interpreted Chris Brown's anger toward Rihanna. She didn't trust him and therefore was checking his text messages. In a lot of cases the man is quite disappointed to find that his committed love has some apprehension.

Now let me give it to you straight, with no chaser. Commitment has a different meaning for a woman than it does for most men. To women, it means security, freedom, loyalty, marriage and it means forever or permanent. To a man, that same word – commitment – means he can't protect himself from you. It means he has to expose his vulnerable side. It means he loses his freedom, his ability to make decisions for himself or his ability to control the emotional roller-coaster ride that follows. But this is where I can be most helpful in suggesting that ladies need to change their tactics and their thinking. Quit telling him to stand up, be a man and marry you. It's not necessarily true that we are weak. We may just be happy with our lives at the time and don't want to introduce possible complications by saying something stupid like... I do! The more you pressure a man about marriage before he is ready, the more apprehensive he becomes. Please don't get upset with me – I'm just the messenger.

If this sound like food for thought, it is. Remember what Shakespeare said: *To thine own self be true*. If you can do that, if you can live it, people will accept you and trust you based on your integrity and actions. The attitude you choose to put forth has everything to do with the response you receive in return. As you become more familiar with your own emotions, you will become more confident in yourself. You will be happy within your own skin and in your heart, never mind what a man says, thinks or does. You will control your destiny; this attitude is very contagious to others.

Tease the confident guy and compliment the shy one. Men don't get compliments often; a genuine compliment about his thoughtfulness will go a long, long way. And one other secret tip for you: Do you know what really sparks a flame in a man? *Anticipation*. We love not knowing how something is going to turn out, the thrill of gradually having the excitement unfold before us. This is the reason men get so fired up about sports... it's the anticipation. So keep your mystery about you. Do not give a man everything right away, or all the time. We love to have a surprise every once in a while or something good to look forward to especially *if it comes from you*! Offer to help out with projects he is devoted to. You will know you are *learning him* when you're able to think ahead for him. There is something binding about a person who is willing to help you with a project that is close to your heart.

Marriage may be overrated but good relationships are priceless. Some of the most powerful women in the world – women who lead their respective industries or professions – are single. And whether you are man-strung, man-less or going about your man in a one-day-at-a-time, take-it-as-it-comes kind of way, you are prone to taking uneducated risks unless you master the formula for *learning* him, in order to truly and deeply *earn* him. So, read on, OK? Nothing you thought you knew has properly prepared you for what I am about to say.

2

The Only Love There Is... Is the Love We Make

The mystery — the magic — the moments

Ladies, I want to empower you with a plethora of information about the way men think, from an Ardent Bachelor's perspective. You may now deem this book your passport; the key that unlocks the mysteries of a man's head and heart. And the best way to win a man's heart is to find out what's in it. One of the main reasons I wanted to write a book on relationships is because of my own peculiar behavior around the idea of commitment. Even though I've been in a couple of long-term relationships, I haven't seriously considered marriage since I got my heart broken more than thirty years ago.

Granted, my profession places me in front of a variety of women who seek my expertise for their image alterations. Sometimes a day's work can fulfill all the needs I may have for communicating with women. As a public servant to women for a living (and this is really how I think of my work!), I can get my "social fix" right at the "office," which is to say, the salon.

This also means one of the pleasures available to me is that, upon returning home, there are no requirements for me to talk or get bossed around. At home, I want to enjoy a relationship built on trust, great anticipation, minimal talking and more pleasures. Regardless of whether it's right or wrong, it's important to know what turns you on and what you want from a companion. Otherwise, you'll spend exorbitant amounts of time looking for excuses to end or bring closure to the relationship. I'm sure you know men who can come up with all types of excuses.

I thought about all the friends (ladies and men) whom I have, and decided to solicit them for information by conducting a national survey at my website, www.barryfletcher.com. I wanted to ask followers on my website their opinion regarding the line of demarcation; the location of that point where things start to get "too serious" between a man and a woman. Is it something a woman does to spook a man? I've heard quite a bit about men disappearing, making misleading gestures and exhibiting cruel treatment. Now I see what you ladies have to go through to get emphatically clear answers out of a man.

As I began writing this book I talked to mature men and women of diverse backgrounds; they were single, divorced, married, sexy, desirable, etc. It took much more effort to get follow-up information out of men than it did women. First you have to track them down, and then it was challenging to pry information out of them without them feeling they were "incriminating" themselves. On the other hand, the women were eager to express themselves and were much more descriptive. Most of the women I spoke with seemed to enjoy talking about their past and present companions. Some could easily be perceived as scorned, while some were disgruntled and upset. But most importantly I heard quite a few success stories. They spoke with redeeming emotions that were calming to their spirits, and also obviously rode along on a wave of feelings. Some of these women told me they could no longer blame themselves for his irrational behavior... behavior they described as inconsiderate and rude. I've heard it all, from women who reported having the best husband in the world to stories of abandonment and infidelity, of betrayal and theft and even of a man having two families and two names. I've heard from women who were misled to believe their man was an ideal man; he told her he wanted a future with her but in actuality he wasn't sure what he wanted.

I learned at a young age that love is nothing to play with. I've had my feelings hurt every time I fell deeply in love, becoming possessive, intrusive, prone to lacking self-confidence, and feeling uncertain and shaky. As hard as I fell for my first love, I didn't like the way she made me feel about myself. She gave me a complex about my looks, my size, my car, my talent, my finances and most of all, my ability to please her. It seemed as if I could never do enough to please her. Being that I was also starting a career that required much of my time, let's just say there were many moments of conflict. I suppose the key point to this story is that after she confessed to cheating on me with her previous boyfriend, it just confirmed all my insecurities! Freak!

A man wants to be the breadwinner in the family without having his thoughts mired with lust and doubt. Many times I have spoken with guys who have confessed to spending too much time with a relationship rather than spending more on career building. Relationships mature with time just like people do. Women have a tendency to be disappointed when they can't get a man's full attention in a relationship, which causes some to give an ultimatum – either you want all of me or none at all.

Inevitably, at some point in your life, you will find that you have some type of need for a man. You just can't live without us. Fact is, we are irreplaceable, no matter how many so-called replacement toys you may buy out of anguish. Anecdotally and boastfully, you discuss with girlfriends your successes and failures with men; proudly analyzing and dissecting, fearing and braving, chuckling and complaining, revealing a torrent of carnal truths amongst friends like dirty jokes. Ladies often engage in this kind of man-related banter as a way of entertaining yourselves, sometimes even in public. In my business, I've heard ladies offering vivid details of a man's inadequacies, and then turn right around and give rave reviews about his sexual prowess. Men on the other hand brag about their swag and the game used on their last romantic or sexual conquest, while exaggerating their macho façade. But when they get home to their partners, the spirit of love takes over... something they don't talk about as much amongst themselves.

There are lots of thoughts going on in a man's head that you'll never know about. So let me tell you at least some of them. I've found that men are more comfortable sharing their thoughts and feelings about women with another male, whereas women are more inclined to run to their girlfriends for advice about their "Boo." In many cases, they both would be better served if they talked to someone of the opposite sex, or if they endeavored to collect information from both sides. For example, you wouldn't go to Senator John McCain for information on rap music, nor would you seek out Lil Wayne for helpful background on domestic policy issues. So why do you only go to your crew of other ladies, in a quest to find out about men? Your search for answers should be focused closer to the source. If you have a trusted male friend, why not tap him for info on the romantic male interest in your life?

What's amazing is the amount of time both sexes spend thinking about their relationship or potential companions. I would estimate that men and women spend at least ten percent of their time thinking about love, sex, romance and dating, investing probably much more than that if they're not satisfied. Men spend quite a bit of this time deciphering gender-specific "Morse code," trying to figure out if "she loves me; she loves me not." Guys seem to shield their hearts more than women, probably because women get more opportunities to reject men and crush their egos; mostly because of the mixed signals you all send out.

I can remember times hanging out with the fellas at the go-go club. We'd spot a little hottie across the dance floor. My boys would say something like, "She's over there dancing for you Fletch," which only confirmed my suspicions about her interest in me. I see a young lady over there dancing in her seat, and my ego suggests that now is a good time to pull her, gotta show the boys how it's done. We lock eyes for a moment, prompting me to move her way. She watches me walk all the way across the dance floor to ask her to dance... only to give a resounding, head-swiveling, "No, I don't want to dance." I freeze for a moment but then think... my boys are watching. So I try to talk to her for a minute, to play it off. I lean in to get closer to her ear, and she pulls back from me in disgust. I start thinking about that long trip back across the dance floor to face my boys and 'nem.

Then there's the sexy lady in the grocery store who keeps staring and smiling at us until we approach her... only to find out she's married. This of course makes us wonder, just how married is she? We also have to be aware of the needy chick. She will get fresh with us to make her man jealous. She wants something from him that doesn't have anything to do with sex. Her flirting with us is merely a device to get him to fall in line. Hey, I'm here to tell you, we do not hate the players or the game, but men are hardening their hearts in preparation for those hypnotic, psychic powers women exude when they want their way.

A man will spend an astronomical amount of time trying to figure out the next move of an aggressive woman, hoping she wants to enjoy the same things from a relationship as he does. Women express themselves in subtle ways that are open to interpretation. We never can be too sure which interpretation is accurate and congruent with her goals or intentions. Nothing a good old-fashioned walk in the park wouldn't cure, huh?

But it really depends on what the woman is feeling. A walk in the park could be like walking through the minefields of Iraq. You just never know when things are going to blow up. For these reasons, men are quite apprehensive about opening up and sharing their innermost feelings. Men adopt a defensive posture when it comes to love. If they've experienced the heartbreak and pain of rejection, marriage failure or loss of a good friend, they will try to protect their vulnerability by appearing to be strong and independent.

Just because a man doesn't say he's in love with you, doesn't mean he isn't. Love isn't always peaches and cream, cuddly and sweet. To a man love is more action than emotions. Measure a man's love for you by his sacrifices. If he gives up watching games with the fellas, takes off frequently from work to be with you; if he gives you the remote, lets you pick out the movies; if he submits to your request for errands and chores, he's whipped. Men usually aren't that selfless when it involves their time, space and freedom. My experiences have given me many opportunities to dissect and inspect human thoughts and sensitivities. Men naturally assume a posture of calm, whereas women seem to be more expressive. For that reason, I'm not sure if women have a clue as to how strong and overwhelming a man's sex drive can be. It actually consumes a great deal of our physical, emotional and mental capacity.

I think some of the issues surrounding the way we see love come from this fundamental difference: Women actually love the *man*, while, in a lot of cases, men love the way a woman *makes him feel*. If he tells you he loves you during sex, that's just what he means; and that'll be enough to keep him. Love is what you make it, so don't sit around and wait for it to hit you like a surge from a good drug. I submit to you: love is just as much about our actions as it is about the person. And for that reason, a man fears he won't be good enough, as he tries to top his last performance. Ladies, if you want to keep love on the high note, show enthusiasm, show him you really want him, that you crave him with eager anticipation. He'll do what he has to do to make sure his equipment works, so that he will continue to keeping your fire burning!

Ask yourself, "What sacrifices would you be willing to make in order to have the man of your dreams?" Would it be important to have a very talkative man? Or could you give up the affable, gregarious side of him? How about your fashions, or the big fancy house, or children? Can you live without a brand-new car? Or are you the type who has to have it all? Some of you are reading this and probably thinking, "I want a man who can give me all of this because that's what I deserve." And you're probably right. But you also should know that this kind of pressure on a man is what contributes to dousing the flames of love or cause a man to stop trying to live up to this expectation or standard.

Brothers are trying to put love on layaway, and some are saving for love right now. Reality is this... some brothers would rather spend money buying some of the best love there is... the kind we can call our own. I'm sure that statement won't win any popularity contests, but let me put one more thing on your mind. It takes a fool to learn that love don't love nobody. Now then, the next time you scan your computer looking for a dating site, someone to talk to who is funny and bright, a person who can take you to ecstasies and new heights, you must clearly understand the source of your plight.

Keep in mind that men are looking as well. Assisting a woman with the production of a sexual climax is one of the most exhilarating, uplifting, powerful experiences known to man. If the man exercises good timing, both of you can go for a blast! It's like being on Apollo 13 heading to the moon... what a lift! When you do it with someone you really care for, now that's **love baby**. The dues a man will pay for love are astronomical, placing the woman in debt with him quite rapidly because men pay to receive; coloring the debts the woman incurs as fair. In all fairness, most guys, if presented with an opportunity to just have sex or the chance to meet the love of their life, would choose to meet the love of their life. That said, the true measurement of a man's love is expressed by how he loves, protects, educates and raises his children. I am talking about the *storge* kind of love, which refers to familial love, the kind you can reach out and touch, not just an inner feeling. (I explain more about the various types of love in Chapter 14.) A woman can take credit for influencing a man's love, but where his offspring are concerned, he'll be responsible for influencing them.

There are bad, good, better and best times to come into a man's life, and he may not even know when those times are. Weakened by your influence, he may let you in any old time. There's also such a thing as investing in one's potential, you'll have to weigh out the pluses and minuses on your own. We all want somebody to love and when we find somebody to love, we must take our time with them. Men want to know you want them for who they are and not for the lifestyle. What really endures as couples get older is not sex or love, but friendship. That's not to say we don't care about sex when we're older. We want you to get yours for as long as possible! However, the man has more control of himself when he practices lovemaking with regularity. Men understand there are different stimulation techniques that vary from female to female. The main objective is to please you in any way; therefore, most men are open to suggestions if it will assist you in reaching the height of orgasm.

Here are some of the things you might want to consider in your quest to achieve equal opportunity lovemaking: desire, foreplay, moisture, protection, pressure, weight, scent, sounds, lighting, location, speed and mutual timing. When partners coordinate these elements of personal comfort, they can successfully reach the formula of variables that turn *sex* into *lovemaking*.

I was once told by a young lady, during one of my book review social gatherings, what she believed were the proper steps to keep a man from straying. She insisted that all a woman has to do is orally satisfy her man and he won't leave you. Now granted, I'm in no position to argue with the woman (smile)... I'm just not sure if she was totally correct, although I do think it's worth a try! When I surveyed the men about this lady's theory, most agreed sex was the motivating factor for infidelity; however, it wasn't the only factor. They confessed to me that the full array of the attention they were given, the compliments, romance, intrigue, the newfound excitement of a "fresh look," is what brought on urgency and incurable anticipation. They also admitted it wasn't worth getting caught and ruining the love and trust they had established with their spouse or significant other. It wasn't worth the separation, the divorce, splitting up everything, confusing the kids, moving out and starting over. That would explain the power of sex, but none of these things would happen if there was a presence of mental, spiritual and intellectual love. Couples struggle more with only having physical rather than emotional love.

Making up is sometimes hard to do, but it is the one thing that will cause a relationship or loving partnership to become stronger. Whether you call it a make-up apology, make-up hug, or make-up love, there's nothing like make-up sex. And ultimately, the act of making up your mind is the most important goal: Is your love worth saving? Nevertheless, love doesn't make the world go round. Sex makes the journey all the more enjoyable. Sex is the reward for love. Love me like we've loved each other for years; surprise me like we just met!

3

Boys to Men

From arrested development to
knight in shining armor to
hero

As an infant, a boy is an active fount of energy and joy. He is willing to learn, inquisitive and playful. At this phase, he can be taught easily and he yearns for knowledge. He's cheerful, friendly, and as he grows up to be a toddler, likes to ask questions. In most cases he is, at this point, also a good listener. With the proper guidance, education, encouragement, positive influences and challenges, any boy can grow up to be one fine young man.

We live in a day and age when many boys are raised overwhelmingly by women, with little regular or no interaction with their biological father or even with a father figure. The family structure as we once knew it – with Dad at the head of the table and the primary breadwinner, and Mom staying home to care for Brother and Sis – is largely no longer in existence. Sure, there are still two-parent households and definitely there are still strong men heading those households, but how prevalent are they? What happened to this model, and why? And what's happening to our children as this model fades away? How is this new dynamic affecting them and society as a whole? What pattern is emerging, and is it positive?

From the moment of birth we are mimicking what we observe and learn from our experiences and the people around us. Good, bad, or indifferent, we are products of our environment. In this context, I want to focus a bit on our boys and how we bring them to fruition as men. What is a boy and what is a man? In between, there are teens – those not quite boys, not quite men characters, who are always busy with something or other. Sometimes, men get stuck within the teenage phase – call it arrested development – and may never learn to take on adult responsibilities; therefore, somehow they do not transition or cross over to manhood.

There's a difference between nature and nurture as it relates to a child's ability to make good choices in their own decisions. You can easily spot the boy who has been carefully nurtured by the way he takes careful consideration in advance of making an important decision. This book is about helping ladies understand the psyche of men. If we are to raise the standard by which we judge men, then we must train and teach our boys to grow to become high quality, substantive men.

Let's get right to it. Raising a son without the required benefits of having a father or a father figure on the premises is the primary trepidation about a healthy environment. Bottom line – a boy must learn from a man, just as much as he must learn from a woman. And ideally, he will learn from not just any man but from a good, strong man of excellent moral character. Many thanks to those women who are "doing the damn thing" and raising their sons as best they can, and in many cases grooming them to be fine young men.

Indeed, my hat is off to you! I have nothing but love for you! But I also have to share that the manly characteristics you are striving to impart to your son – and again, your efforts are greatly appreciated – will inevitably come from a woman's perspective... because that is who you are. This means that the boy may still lack the necessary manly touch, which is to say, the manly psyche that is necessary to influence the future full and mature development of a man. So if the boy's biological father or a father figure is willing and available to spend time with him in his formative years, it is worth it for you to consider letting your boy hang out with him – as long as he is a good man – as often as possible. For all the love and sincere effort women bring to the task, there is a big difference between *teaching* a boy to be manly, and *sharing with him* what you know from experience, and what you can actually feel it means to be a man.

Ladies, you say you want a good gentleman, a kind sensitive hard-working provider; a passionate lover, a man who is spiritual, and masculine, who takes care of his health, and who, of course, treats his woman as his Queen! But how does a man get there? How does he learn how to do these things? How do we instill these traits in him? The purpose of schooling is to educate us and prepare us to function and succeed in life. The purpose of childhood must be the same. Yes we want our children to learn to play and enjoy their childhood but we also must use teachable moments to ensure they learn life's lessons well. What you learn early in life will affect your quality of life later.

According to some influential learning theorists, one's personality is a collection of learned behavior patterns. The social cognitive approach to personality is determined by one's cognition (thoughts), feelings, values and expectations, topped with what is learned by observing others. Some of a boy's personality is measured by self-efficacy, which is basically the boy's faith in his own ability to behave appropriately, or to produce a desired outcome. Self-esteem, on the other hand, encompasses his positive and negative self-evaluation. Boys are infinitely *changeable, through the process of learning new behavior patterns.* So what are we teaching these boys?

Look at the music videos – and yes I'm going there! Listen to the music itself. What influences are we allowing to permeate our children's minds? Dooney Da Priest has a video out titled, "Pull Your Pants Up!" This video speaks volumes about basic disrespect for self and others that infuses much of our culture today. "Pull Your Pants Up!" is a plea for a return to self-respect.

Do you remember the days when the sight of a scantily-clad girl broadcast on a popular TV program generated a backlash of outrage so loud that the network executives would have no choice but to seriously consider taking the show off the air? I remember when some women's rights groups complained that "Charlie's Angels," a popular network show in the mid-1970s, was leading young women astray by showing three attractive actresses – Farah Fawcett Majors, Jaclyn Smith, and Kate Jackson – wearing skimpy outfits while they solved crimes. And those three "Angels" were really only guilty of sometimes showing a little outline of a nipple through their T-shirts every now and then!

Well, when did we become so permissive and why? How did we get to the point where we will allow our sons (and daughters, for that matter) to watch videos of "club girls" shaking their half-naked butts at the camera, while a rapper pours Cristal between her legs? As parents and adults we swear to each other that we don't want our young ladies looking "common," but who is buying these girls those "Hootchie Mama"-type clothes? Teenage girls rolling out sportin' Daisy Duke-style shorts, tighter than a drum? And just who is letting their boy walk around with his jeans hanging down his ass, so his business pokes out everywhere? Who are the parents allowing her and him to wear this stuff? Who sees this and yet chooses to look the other way?

Young girls go through puberty approximately two years before boys; therefore, they can be more sexually aggressive, mature and astute. Boys have to work harder at being sexual, at least initially. Once, I was speaking with the parent of a young girl, and she shared with me that she had difficulty finding clothing to fit her 13-year-old daughter – seems she kept finding styles that either were too tight or that would barely cover her daughter's knees. Another parent shared with me concerns about her son, a 9-year-old, who had told her that he has a "girlfriend"... and that she was 12 years old. Oh, and he added that he considers himself a *Pimp Daddy* and, in case Mom still did not rec-a-nize, he then proceeded to request clothing with more swagger. Yep. So, I listened to that, and I wondered, "Where did he get that from?"

Some parents share with me concerns that are more troubling. One parent I know, for example, told me she believed that many youngsters today have indeed positively absorbed the "Just Say No," Nancy Reagan-era public service message that doing drugs, or having sexual intercourse before you are "ready" is *bad*. But, before I could start applauding, this parent let me know that the youngsters translated that important message into meaning that oral sex – which some of them call 'bopping' – is a cool alternative to intercourse. Uh, yeah. You parents got some 'splaining to do!

The point is: We grown-ups have an important role to play in all of this. We see our boys wearing the sagging pants, and how crazy it makes them look – but do we say anything to them, or do we just keep our disgust to our selves, and then keep it moving? Not long ago, I was listening to Pastor Joel and Ylawnda Peebles of Jericho Christian Center in Landover, Maryland, on their radio show. They were talking about how Sister Peebles sometimes embarrasses her teenaged daughter whenever she would speak to young men in the vicinity. Ms. Peebles said she calmly and politely communicates with the young men asking them why they are wearing their pants in a manner that allows their underwear to show... and for good measure, she sometimes suggests to them some reasons why they may want to pull them UP. But she made it clear, she was not, at those times, preaching – not condemning; just initiating a friendly conversation. (Although, obviously, such a conversation in this context may leave any daughter blushing and sputtering from embarrassment). But Sis. Peebles got it exactly right. Her approach is, "Come, let us reason together." I say: What's wrong with that? Why can't we share this kind of knowledge with our boys? Why aren't we doing this more often, with our own children, with the neighborhood kids, with your nieces, nephews, and 'nem? But I digress.

We want our boys to be kind and gentle but somehow, the number one selling video game, *Grand Theft Auto,* has as its primary purposes killing, stealing, running folks over, car jacking, and shooting someone – anyone. This game says that it's okay to steal a car. It's even better to outrun the police and get away with it. No problem hitting someone and running them over. Shoot first and ask questions later – or better yet, don't ask questions at all. And many parents today actually allow their boys to become proficient at this game, with the lame defense of 'Oh, well, it is ONLY a game." Well, what's up with that!? How is it that we don't seem to realize that many young men actually internalize the messages they see in pop culture? Nor is it wise if parents keep telling boys that to "be a man" means (exclusively) to be strong, not to be a sissy, to suck it up when he's hurt – don't cry. Man up!

Can I just point out that he's not a man – yet! We want a "gentle man" to emerge in later years, yet as they are forming and learning, we are teaching our boys to be warriors; to be hard; to be strong; to be aggressive – above all and at all costs. I'm going to get you before you can get me. I ain't no punk! I ain't no sissy! I am here to tell you that strength doesn't lie in might nor force alone, but in character, patience, integrity and whether you practice what you preach.

From the onset of puberty, early-maturing boys have an advantage over slower- or later-maturing boys. They are better athletes, more popular and have a more positive outlook at an earlier age. The smaller, less-coordinated boys are less attractive and are more often ridiculed. Just as important as physical change is psychological, social, cognitive and moral development; distinguishing right from wrong and understanding that conflict can exist between two sets of social values. There's a difference between moral judgment and moral behavior. Knowing right from wrong is one thing, the way we act on it is another. Compassionate concerns for the welfare of others represent the highest level of morality. Men generally view morality primarily as broad principles of equal justice and fairness.

We want our boys to be respectful of women – so it is our responsibility to teach them to respect themselves. Too many parents somehow make the mistake of assuming that this is innate knowledge – that we're born knowing this. We don't teach right from wrong anymore – somehow a boy is expected to just know. We need to get back to communicating like we used to. But how can we? We have to compete with a television and sometimes even a computer in every room... in some homes, even in the bathroom and kitchen! We compete with online social networking, with Twitter, Facebook, MySpace, and instant messaging, as if they are an appropriate substitute teacher for life! In too many homes, the dining room is just a show place we pass through; no one eats there and certainly not at the same time! Whatever happened to family dinner time when we would all meet and eat together? We would talk with one another without the interference of the television and radio. We would share our daily experiences and issues and work together to make things better. Is it totally out of the question to get back to that leisurely but valuable time?

So how do we teach our boys to become better men? They must be in the presence of a "better" man. They must see him interact with other men and women. Boys need to see a man open the car door for a woman. He needs to see a man take the hand of and walk with a woman. He needs to see a man spend time and effort looking for the right present to give his woman. A boy needs to talk with a man about how to find a good woman and what are good signs. How do I ask a young lady for a date and what do we do while on it, more importantly, what *NOT* to do. How do I "meet the parents"? What are the signs to notice? How do I pay attention to a woman? He has to see a man be affectionate appropriately with a woman and know that it's not about sex; it's about being respectful.

Pastor Jill Cloud of the Soul Factory, in Forestville, Maryland, and Atlanta, Georgia, shares that when she and her husband, Pastor Deron Cloud, were first dating, she would not even let him hold her hand. She had this rule, initially, because the relationship had not progressed nor developed to that point. She understood that she must demand respect from any man who wanted to be in her presence. She earned that privilege by learning to respect herself first. She knew that, even before she would become a mother, she must set an example and high standards that her daughter – once conceived and born – would observe and follow. A young lady who allows a boy to "hug" her in a full embrace as a supposed "greeting," should not be surprised or alarmed if his hands travel down her back to her hips and beyond. When you allow a "little bit of disrespect," please don't get all twisted, then, if the guy takes advantage and displays more disrespect. There is a time and place for becoming affectionate.

We spend little if any time teaching and demonstrating to our children how you go about showing respect, and how you go about earning it. They can't possibly know what it is to respect someone if they themselves have not been taught what respect is, or witnessed adults or role models around them who conduct themselves always with the utmost self-respect, and respect for others. Likewise, with moral values, boys can't live them if they don't know them, they can't know them if they don't witness them in action.

We wonder why today's children are so quick to fight, can't control their anger, and lash out at the drop of a hat. Maybe boys haven't been taught to value human life. Many boys haven't been taught to reason, verbally, with their adversaries. They haven't been taught tolerance and patience, meekness, love and forgiveness. They haven't been taught to compromise or work things out peaceably. They haven't been taught there are times to fight and times not to fight. And, that if you have to fight, it better be something worth fighting for. Fathers used to tell their sons, "If I find out you've been fighting, your next fight will be with me. So you better make sure it's worth it."

Good quality socialization experiences with parents and other significant adults will enhance a boy's knowledge, values and goals, which will help him function more successfully as an adult. Attitude toward learning is acquired primarily in the home environment. Young parents must realize learning is shaped by the quality of exposure; therefore, a boy's like or dislike toward learning is influenced by his experiences early in life. They are skilled parents who are raising brilliant children in most cases. Fathers who demonstrate loving and caring by nurturing their boys' emotional health and teaching them manners and good behavior are the dads most respected by their children as they mature. The sad reality is that fathers aren't communicating love in a way that boys can easily understand, either because of their absence, limited time or because they themselves don't have the knowledge. As a boy reaches his teen years, a growing need to individualize and become more independent begins to surface.

At the same time, fathers sometimes have a distant way of showing love; by trying to change their son's opinion, discredit his actions or complain about his choices. Deep down inside, every boy has a need for his parent's approval. Behind all the conflict is a desire for his parents to be proud of him, connect with him, give him sincere encouragement and help him grow into manhood. I know it's easier said than done but it is way past time to get away from the idiot box and turn it off for periods of time. Sign off of the Internet and chat rooms and Twitter and MySpace. Socialization has its place; there is a time and place for everything. And there is a time and place to be quiet, study, meditate and just interact with the person right next to you.

For those of you who have boys, try asking them sometimes: Do you know how to change a car tire? How many filters does an engine have, and where are they? If the faucet is leaking what do you do? If the power goes out in one room of the house what does that mean? How do you hang a picture on the wall? Can you throw a curve ball? Which way is up? We used to teach this stuff to our children. What happened? Can we get back to it, please?

Boys need men in their lives. Not just one but several men. Yes, there's a need for men of fine caliber influencing them, and quiet as it's kept – they do exist! Seek out positive activities for our boys and see to it that they include men or older boys who can serve as a positive influence. Maybe it is little league baseball or football or basketball where you'll find some good men. We need more American children playing soccer – the

#1 sport in the world! Find a Boys & Girls Club. Find a recreation center. Some community colleges have programs and classes for young people that afford interaction and blend education as well. Inquire at your child's school about after-school activities. Seek out volunteer opportunities. Every high school requires volunteer service hours.

It is up to you to personally sow wisdom into his life. Share your personal experiences, especially the times you messed up; talk about how mistakes affected your life, and how the goal is not to be "perfect," but to learn from mistakes, and to do your best to not repeat the same mistakes again and again. One of the major injustices we commit is not telling our children how many mistakes we as adults have made in our lives, how many times we had to pay for our mistakes. We hide this knowledge from them because we don't want them to know we were just as stupid back in our day as they are now! And stupid doesn't have to be terminal! Telling youngster, "Do as I say and not as I do" doesn't work, never has, never will. Show that you are human and that you have faults, but that you can recognize them, learn from them and rise above them. Put the time in with him *now* or he may end up serving time later.

I remember a television documentary called *Scared Straight*. I loved it because it gave troubled kids a chance to see where they would end up if their antisocial behavior persisted. In some cases a judge would sentence the child to spend the night in jail as punishment for his behavior. Social workers complained that the experience was too traumatic and disturbing for juvenile delinquents. Back in the day a bandit could go to a correction center or youth facility and learn a trade while getting his head together. Now they just hold them in juvenile jail (juvi-jail) and make them meaner than a pit bull.

Shawn Briggs started out as a mentor with the local agency Family Matters and is now doing community service and foster care for young teens with a great degree of success. He insists that the correctional system should bring back the visits to jail and the subsequent overnight stays. These youngsters need to see it to believe it says Shawn, who is mentoring a young man named Michael, who is going through juvenile correction and has spent time in juvi-jail on his past three birthdays. Under the Briggs' tutelage, Michael has turned his life around. He no longer has problems staying off the block or going to school. He's going to be a leader one day. He's 18 now and will be in the correctional system until he's 21. However, he says, "I'm trapped in the system but free in my mind."

Briggs maintains that there is a need for more male mentors and role models. There just isn't that much going on in terms of rehabilitation these days. There is foster care, as well as group homes, alternative placement services and juvenile service support groups that may offer one-on-one counseling. A strong male role model family member is always good. When all else fails, call the Department of Social Services and Corrections. For the past ten years, the Census Bureau stats for the rate of single parent households have basically remained unchanged: 56 percent for blacks, 32 percent for Hispanics, 26 percent for Native Americans, 24 percent for Asians and 20 percent for whites. Joblessness for 16- to 24 year-old black men reached 34.5 percent in October 2009, more than three times the rate for the general U.S. population (10.2 percent). The national joblessness rate for all 16-to-24-year-olds was 19.1 percent.

Mothers have been trying to be stricter on their sons to help make up for not having a man in the household; allowing them to watch videos only in the summer, cutting their hair short if they start to act thuggy because it's long, exposing them to diversity, helping them avoid idle time, getting them mentoring in church and with male fellowship groups. Sometimes a kid just needs some holistic street counseling or an unconditional friend. They don't care if you have a degree or not. At times it's about listening to another voice and a different perspective. Lean on the Boys Club of America, the Big Brother Organization, the J.R.O.T.C, the armed services, The Alliance of Concerned Black Men, Sasha Bruce Mentoring Agency or The Peace a Holics. Check in your city for mentoring groups. We have got to get more involved with our children's upbringing, whether they're ours or not. Otherwise they'll grow up with a grave disregard for life, fearless in all the wrong ways.

I have to agree with Steve Perry, principal and founder of Capital Preparatory Magnet School in Hartford, Connecticut. He writes in the December 2009 issue of Essence magazine:

The Black community is raising thugs: poorly developed, undereducated, lethal little boys. They are our sons, nephews, cousins and babies' fathers. They are the drug dealers and murderers in our neighborhoods. We've built homes for these unchecked, unloved young men who live for the moment, and hurt and hurt until yet another honor student's blood stains our conscience. Perry says our acceptance of 'thug culture' makes all of us a part of the problem.

He was responding to the death of Derrion Albert, a 16-year-old boy who was beaten to death by a black teenage mob in Chicago – a city where 40 kids had been killed by the end of 2000. Perry also says we shouldn't use violence as the primary method of disciplining children in our homes. Our children will change when we do.

The greatest gift of age is wisdom and perspective. Perspective is what we recognize as wisdom, which is obtained by living and then looking back to reflect. Nowhere is it more needed than in parenting teens; at that time, for parents, wisdom and perspective also must be combined with another precious commodity – patience. Parents will go through societal pendulum swings. But they should always try to remember that those who love their children will win.

Loving parents ride out the storm of their tumultuous teens evolving into men. We all know that raising a boy in today's society is not easy and that defining manhood for boys is even harder. It seems that sometimes a parent's work is never done. He will need help with his selection of vocations, sports, career choices, travel, finances, driving, personal hygiene, fashion, guy friends – and girlfriends. One day, as his adolescence turns to teen-hood, you'll have to sit him down and tell him all about that "fast" 15-year-old girl down the street. You can talk with him about drugs and peer pressure. And just when you think you've taught him all he needs to know, you will encounter the hardest part of being a smart parent: knowing when to let him go.

4

A Woman's World

Men are just squirrels trying to get a nut

Women, particularly mothers, have an overwhelming influence on the lives of men. That influence has its roots in molding sons' imaginations, forming sons' emotions and indirectly shaping sons' actions. The way I see it, any young man who takes the time to know himself without the help of a woman is more likely to learn to be confident about his decisions, and more likely to be able to make big plans without depending on another's approval.

I speculate that a large number of men never break free of women. Therefore, they risk never defining manhood through their own experiences and may continue to deny, react or fight against the control and primal power that women have over them. Men continue to live with this subconscious notion of never getting in touch with their deepest, truest innermost feelings. What is taboo to men and often not known is the extent to which our lives revolve around our relationships with a woman. She is our nucleus, our mystery, the place where we manifest our feelings; the actress, the stage and the audience by which the drama of our life is displayed. The fragility of a man's psyche is in continual danger because it's so deeply rooted in the way we were raised. Our feelings, thoughts, vision, emotions, spirit and impressions of the world are braided together by our mother and teacher.

As newborns, we are programmed by face recognition and spend most of our waking hours focused usually on Momma and the many changing aspects of her face, from smiling to laughing to frowning. Soon we learn how to read her expressions to the point of knowing in a second if she thinks you've been bad or good, when it is time to eat, sleep, walk, talk or go to the bathroom. Think about the intellectual and emotional fundamentals we learned before we were even weaned.

I happen to believe, in a strange esoteric way, that my fascination for breasts is somehow connected to my experience with them as a lil' young'un. When you think about it, a mother's breast is like a computer that programs your reasoning with life, while her face is like a computer monitor. I've learned many lessons while online and sometimes with getting connected. When I was an infant, my mom used her own kind of dial-up connection to get me online. She would take a while getting herself together, and make sure nobody was looking when she hooked me up to her breast – my earliest computer was at last connected and humming along! After I got older and started demanding that computer, she switched over to high-speed DSL. She would pull that computer out just about anywhere and flip it on, whether we were in church or in the grocery store...bam! Now let me get serious – my point is that when you're on the breast, you learn to receive nourishment, desire, satisfaction, judgment, temperament, expectation and a little attitude. The mother's body is the first source of information, a learning tool. We found comfort in those warm, sensuous, loving arms. We learned to trust her and feel secure. We also learned about fear and danger when those arms weren't there to comfort us.

Mothers will always have dominion over man even as adults, because she wordlessly taught us some of our most valuable lessons. She shaped us before we even knew how to speak the language. It was our mother who pre-programmed our life – teaching us manners, sensitivity, how to think and what to think. She was our tour guide into adulthood. All the way up to my mother's final days, I sought her approval and feared her disappointment. In April 2009, I remember practicing over and over again trying to please her by singing her a song while playing the piano for Mother's Day. It meant the world to me to do that for her, so I made sure I got my brother Ronnie and cousin Tiny, who could really sing, to be my backup singers. I'm happy to say it went well. Trust me, if you think you love her now, you'll love her more than you can ever imagine when she's gone.

So in the context of such an important early teacher – our Momma – I will tell you where the burden lies for a man. It arrives when he is trying to find himself, his identity and how he wants people to perceive him – and he isn't sure how to do it, or if he wants to sever the umbilical cord from his mother. I always wanted to make my mother proud of me, and in my early years my mother and older sisters were my role models. Shortly after reaching my teens, I remember wanting to be more like my Dad. He dressed like a celebrity and had a nice car. He could go out anytime he wanted but my mother couldn't. This was the time in my life when I saw Pops exercise power and authority. That was the beginning of my transitional phase of admiring a male role model while trying to find my manhood. Meanwhile, I had to develop a strategy to finesse myself away from my mother's powers, not knowing that this was a time that required some important judgment: Do you become a Momma's Boy, a baller, the class clown or a bookworm? Do you spend the rest of your life trying to please your mother and win her approval, or make your own decisions about your social life and your attractions to girls?

Mind you, this is the time when young girls have gone through puberty and are often more aggressive than boys. The girls are the ones who teach young boys about the birds and the bees. My dumb butt, I didn't know anything about sex. I would take my girl up to the hayloft on our farm and we'd rub on each other. I didn't know anything about penetration until she showed me. I remember saying "It goes in there? Eeeewww, yuck!" But I've got to tell you, after the first time she drained my little lizard, I knew there was something special about girls. And I'm still learning more and more every day.

I've been sucking on a woman's breast from the first time I opened my eyes, but I don't get as many nutrients now as I did when I was a little pup. Nevertheless, my knowledge of the benefits of this still gives me a major connection with women. I'll never forget how, after I grew old enough to figure out what to do with a woman's breast, I discovered that they had two of them! But first I had to break free from my mother to make myself available for another woman, which in turn, helped me begin to understand manhood and appreciate motherhood. I learned quickly that women have mystical, spiritual, erotically charged and irresistible powers and that some women will use these powers to control men without them realizing it.

To Christians, God is perceived as "Father," and so it is that most American men consider themselves made in His image, at least in the context of being Lords of the land, of Mother Nature and of their homes. In anthropological terms, historically we have defined men as "active" and the woman as "reactive" or "responsive" or "passive." But if you think about it, even in that biblical framework that equation has always had contradictions, right? Because as we most certainly learned from the Bible, that "passive" woman, "active" man thing wasn't so true with Adam and Eve was it? In actuality, it's the female gender that sends out her scent or pheromones, which invites the male in for action or mating. This in effect makes her the initiator, or the "actor" who motivates the man toward action. This is a basic, biological means for woman to use her unspoken powers to get men moving. From that fundamental basic truth we arrive at contemporary times and have to admit that it remains a woman's world... and that we men are just squirrels trying to get a nut.

A man subconsciously craves that a woman tell him how big his manhood is, which translates directly to how large his ego will be. The man expresses power through his angelic or demonic exercising of his sexuality; these are the biological powers that he controls, and he has to learn about that power and how to use it, separate from his mother's influence. I believe some young men are better served by separating themselves from their mother and girlfriend long enough to allow them the opportunity to learn their purpose, direction or journey. The young man's sexual power is not going to be his only or most useful power throughout his entire life. But he needs to figure out how power works relatively early, and most adolescent boys will experience a swift, urgent need to learn how to control and wield that first hint of hormonal power. If they can successfully manage the first "rush" of that particular sexual power, they will gain confidence that will mature over time. A young man needs time to figure out who he really is as a man. He needs to learn how to think for himself, with himself, and learn the joys of solitude without being incarcerated.

Whenever I started to wander away from whatever game plan my mother had for me as a teen, she would threaten to send me to Cheltenham, a boys' correctional center in Maryland. You best believe it would straighten me up every time! I would get serious about school again, or about the tasks at hand. But looking back, I sometimes wonder if it would have done me any justice; the time away from my parents and friends might have actually been beneficial for me... would it have gotten me more focused earlier in my life?

That could very well be the key to unlocking the mystery of manhood: coming up with a way to isolate young men for at least a period of time... and not necessarily in a jail, either! Ladies, I'm sure many of you would agree, the majority of these young punks walking the streets today need to *man-up* and figure out manhood in its most mature regards, not just in the superficial, pants-hangin'-down, gimme-some-respect-or-I'ma-F-you-up kind of fronting that we see many of the youngsters getting caught up in. I personally wonder if some of these young guys have ever really figured out how to separate from their mothers, and if instead, they are *imitating* manhood without really experiencing the fullness and confidence that comes from *owning* your manhood.

For a guy to establish a clear, present, and realistic kind of manhood, he must lose the fear of women – the fear that she someday may not be there to hold his hand – and learn to make decisions which elevate his caliber. I've seen it played out numerous times in the movies... where the gangster who has made some bad decisions and gotten away with murder (just like some of these kids on the street) then decides he wants to turn his life around and leave his past behind. So he takes his girlfriend with him, not knowing where they're going... and winds up getting them both killed. On the other hand, a cowboy who has just shot up several people in self defense tells his lady that he's leaving town – alone – to get his life together and promises to come back and get her, then tells her he loves her. He leaves, finds work, establishes himself, builds a safe haven of a home, then he goes back to town, fetches his future wife and lives happily ever after. The moral of these Hollywood archetypes: define who you are and what your journey will be before you decide who is going to accompany you.

Nowadays, in the real world, we see instances in which a young man decides to leave his mother for the first time to join the Army. The first thing he wants to do is get married, which is like surrendering his soul for a woman's approval before he has truly given himself the chance to live alone within himself. It is a sure sign of what I would call a young man who is *ill at ease* with himself. Regardless of whether you think it is a good or bad decision, I personally think this choice to go from Momma directly to a wife is just too risky a commitment, in terms of how it limits his opportunity to really get to know himself. In some ways, it can also limit his ability to completely control his own life. Let's put it this way. If you marry a young man who is leaving home to become a man, how do you know *what kind* of man will come back home to you?

But hear me now – this is all the fault of you women! (Said with love ladies, only with love!) Some of you say you want a strong, committed, wealthy, smart, good-looking, Mandingo Warrior type. Then you rush him into marriage, not considering this important question: How well does he know himself? Now tell me how can you help him do better for himself, if you are getting in the way of his goals and dreams... goals and dreams that he hasn't even thought up yet? That's just what he needs, another woman to make his mind up for him.

I'll tell you what's even sadder. The man you're hooked on could be suffering symptoms of all the uncertainty he feels, and suffering from them right now! If he seems distant, or angry, or too quiet for no apparent reason, this may be the cause! That said, I know there are plenty ladies who get this. And I want to take this time right now to thank all the women who have helped men be all they could be, even if it didn't result in a personal benefit. Thank you! After all, men just want to do better so that we can please you better, Baby. 'Cause at the end of the day, a man still needs a place for his head to lay... and most times, he prefers it to be right next to a lovely lady.

There's nothing more alluring than the love of a woman to make a man put his feelings on the line. It's up, it's down and that might not be as bad as it may sound... because there ain't nothing we can't work out over a bottle of wine. What I'm telling you is – it is a woman's world, girl! And it wouldn't be nothing – NOTHING – without a man acting like a squirrel!

5

The Actions of Attraction

The thrill of the chase can lead to a journey of love

Attraction is one of the most fascinating social factors of the selection process. This first impression phase is based on physical appearance: body shape, curves, bumps and proportions. Closer contact gives us an opportunity to scan the smile, eyes, skin and most importantly hair!

Look deep into your intended's eyes to read the landscape and determine if the lust is mutual. Physical characteristics tantalize a man's sensitivity and appeal to his aesthetic sensibility. As the Commodores famously sang it, "36-24-36, she has the winning hand, 'cause she's a brick house." Nevertheless, we've moved up to building mansions since that record first became a hit, "moved on up to the east side and finally got a piece of the pie." Bigger is supposed to be better these days. Regardless of your thirst or hunger, it is all about more abundance. Going out with a model type is not always the plight of the prowl on the prairie.

But then there are always the unconscious factors, those elements that we are sometimes unaware of. What attracts us to the opposite sex? Perhaps we are attracted to someone who fulfills our needs and makes us feel good about ourselves, boosts our ego or offers financial support. As strange as this may sound, some people are attracted to those who are down and out; those who are helpless, handicapped or having problems taking care of themselves. It's just the nurturing side of a woman.

Dating traditions and customs are influenced by cultural and family values and beliefs, which could be beneficial or detrimental depending on your objectives for the relationship. Let's go back a century to a time when a man who desired a woman and wanted to court her had to first meet her family formally and obtain permission to take their daughter out. Can you imagine this type of practice today? In most cases a man doesn't want a woman to meet his mother unless it's very serious. The mother normally never objects and the only problem he'll have is finding his dad. The young girls today don't want to bring their boyfriend home for fear of traumatizing their parents. He walks in reeking of weed, sporting several tattoos, got funky hair, a face piercing and his pants are down to his knees. The young lady's mother is wondering what in hell his plans are for her daughter. She may even be thinking she would be more comfortable with someone of another race or gender!

Thug-love: It's a problem with young ladies who are trying to find themselves these days. The so-called nice guys who are sensitive, caring, patient and thoughtful, appear to be the favorite of older women. However, young ladies seem to prefer men who are aggressive, dominant, confident and thug-like. These are the brothers who are having the most sexual success. Why is that? I'll let you ladies ponder how and why the thugs are getting their groove on.

Life is a journey of love and learning. I've found that some people don't want to learn or grow from their experiences. They just want a mate who will commit to them at any cost or sacrifice, overlooking any previous relations or bad marriages. As a result, they continue to endure the misfortunes of unsuccessful relationship. The chemistry of attraction is so strong that people will sacrifice their integrity to satisfy a need. The sexual power in a relationship is so influential that he takes a part of you with him when it's good, causing you to crave his presence so that he may put that part back in you making you whole again. It's hard to control an attraction because it appears clear and urgent, right in front of you and that's amazing in itself. A man's emotions will sometimes overcome him, making him say silly things, make kind gestures or stare at you like you're from hell... all the while the front of his pants swell.

If attracting a man is your mission, you should never leave your home without putting on something that makes you look and feel good. I can't help but think about a client of mine who's been looking for a man for the past four years. Lately she considers herself celibate. She worries the hell out of me about her hair, wanting every strand to be in place. In the meantime she's wearing a pair of jeans that make her look like the coal-miner's daughter! They were high-wasted to cover her stomach. Worse, she tops them with a thick black biker-belt that your momma might have used to chase you and your brothers and sisters around the house with, threatening to whip your butts.

When I commented about her attire, she assured me she was going right home and taking them off. My suggestion was to not only take them off, but throw them away! You never want to wear anything that could cause you any sexual deprivation, especially if you're looking for some.

That's right, attraction – a "many-splendored thing" – could be the reason why you have so many choices. If you want men to rain on you, start with the fact that we like sexy and beauty on all levels. Wear clothes that show off your favorable attributes. Give men the opportunity to notice you. This will encourage them to pursue you and find out what's on your mind and in your heart. In other words, he's not going to ask you out if he's not attracted to you and you never know when or where he might spot you.

Some of you should think about changing your paradigm of how you see yourself, perhaps by getting help from pros and friends: personal fitness instructor, personal image consultant, skin and makeup consultant, and nutrition specialist. Get your teeth cleaned and whitened, then come see me for a hair makeover. In some cases it may only require you asking a friend you respect for their style and fashion tips, to help you go through your wardrobe, to guide you as you throw out all the clothing that doesn't enhance your appearance or new image. Give your old garments away to charity or family members, and then go shopping for clothes that flirt for you. I've always liked fabrics that feel soft like your skin. Feeling good to the touch is important. The closer I get to you through contact, the greater the degree of allure you hold for me. Try some new personal appearance preparations and you just might experience not running from the rain for a change... because the next time it rains it could be storming men. No matter how many men you have a casual relation with, your actions of attraction will confirm your desire for love, affection and opportunity.

Also ladies, this is important: It could be your own behavior that is keeping you single! Be honest with yourself about what you think you truly deserve or who you think you really are. If your personal truth is mired in doubts, distrust, shamefulness or lies, it will show through in subtle nonverbal ways. You don't have to be all the things that you think might make you more attractive. Just be genuine and someone will love you for it, if you know what that is. Confidence and self-acceptance says you're sold on your product, and your product just happens to be you. Most men can sense desperation. Desperation is like a strong scent in the air for all hound dogs to smell. It's like spoiled meat in the trap that makes them run like hell.

Personally, I've never looked for love and therefore felt that it would just have to happen for me. However, there is such a thing as falling in love on purpose. Be careful about "falling" in love. The term is quite suggestive. It means to drop freely under the influence of gravity; to move oneself to a lower position, to assume an expression of disappointment: to be conquered or overthrown, to drop in status. Wow, that list speaks volumes in terms of falling in love. Yet at the same time, love happens on purpose when you have a strategic plan to attract a man! Exercise patience and learn to control your emotions. The fact that most people are motivated by fear could be the reason some women reek of desperation... a scent that can be detected from miles away. So when you look in the mirror and say to yourself, "I love me and what do I need a man for?" My response is, "Guess who loves you more?"

6

The Complexity of Cultivating a Relationship

Effective communication is key,
and most of it is nonverbal

The quest for intimacy reigns supreme in the world of socializing and human connection. Interested parties negotiate complex relational networks by exchanging dialogue without one overpowering the other. The use of dating sites is extremely popular today, giving individuals an opportunity to expose themselves to a plethora of choices. You bring the line, he'll bring the pole, you'll go fishing and surfing worldwide... by yourself, looking for someone to share yourself with, exercising options for yourself. You're free to roam, hear the sound of freedom, type in the spirit of liberation! If you're not happy with the types of guys you are attracting, dating sites can offer a quick and relatively easy way to present yourself to guys who may be your ideal match.

Do you fill out your profile fictitiously to attract the man you desire, or do you pour out your heart and reveal the true you? Which photos would be appropriate to send the right message? How should you position your status and stature? It's important to know what you're looking for if finding your ultimate mate is important to you. The more serious you are about finding your soul mate, the more honest you need to be about the information you send out. I won't recommend any specific sites but I advise you that it is important to choose a safe place to meet for the first time. Profiles and photos can be changed to protect the innocent. However, people are generally experiencing quite a bit of success with online dating.

In a world of stature and status, independence adds a little swagger and clout to your plight. I think it's safe to say that both sexes need intimacy *and* freedom. Men tend to focus on the latter and consequently this is where negotiations are at an all-time premium. Communication will definitely highlight the differences in beliefs and yield opportunities for endearment. The magic of communication is uninhibited, a constant balancing act, as we ponder multiple decisions to be made over conflicting desires over romance and finance. Men want to make decisions without discussing them – and we don't want to hear about a woman's decision unless it's going to cost us some money. That's probably the only time a woman won't want to discuss it.

I got to tell you ladies something else important about how men perceive you. Some of the toughest times we spend with you are when we are trapped and have to sit through one of those long drawn-out discussions about a topic we don't care about! It's not that we don't need to hear it. It's just the fact that we can't run from it any longer, making it all the more haunting. Even when you approach a man with a suggestion about obtaining his opinion, he thinks it's a trap to help you make a decision about something that's going to take up a lot of time and there's a chance you've already made your mind up about it anyway. At this time, men realize they have to fasten their seat belts and prepare for turbulence, as a woman begins to request information. Let's be clear, I don't want to run the risk of sounding condescending. I respect the complexity of cultivating a friendship or a romantic interest. We are just as much alike as we are different. We are the "opposite sex" after all.

Both parties are insecure to some extent. A man feels insecure when he doesn't know how to handle a certain situation. This may result in perplexing behaviors as he ponders and hesitates and tries to figure out how to respond. Fear of rejection is another common insecurity. Sometimes an obligatory challenge is a good test. Would the partners instinctively come to the rescue of their significant other in a time of need?

A man can be considered aloof if he is quiet and doesn't care to be in every conversation, and a woman could be considered a nag if she talks too much or repeats herself often. Challenges in a friendship can sometimes be the result of unconscious or unspoken power struggles. A woman may blatantly disregard what she perceives as hierarchy and resist any notion of subordination in the relationship.

As a hair designer, I sometimes wrestle with the authority and power I have in deciding which haircut would be best based on a client's ability to take care of it vs. giving her the high-maintenance, trendy haircut she prefers. There are always underlying dynamics that create some kind of sense out of a senseless disagreement. The meaning or the message in most conversations doesn't reside in the words, but in the attitude, the expression or the actions of the words. Men don't mind actionable info and try to avoid emotional info like it's the swine flu. Men more often want to be the authority in the conversation nevertheless. They will lend you an ear, put you on a timer and then make their point. Some men are challenged by women in the workplace and are quick to defend their territory thinking that women might have a special type of advantage because they are women. Women have been kicking butt in the workplace and gaining political power since the year of the woman in 1992, after the Anita Hill quagmire. We know that President Clinton was very considerate of women, appointing quite a few to his Cabinet. Woman power is growing stronger every day. There was a concern among some men that their power would have taken a hit if Hillary Clinton had become President.

Women are perceived to be smarter than men as a rule. However, because of family commitments, women usually don't put in the same amounts of time that men can devote to their career. At the same time, I happen to believe that "women's liberation" put chivalry in a choke hold decades ago. I disagree that women are from Venus and men are from Mars; we all grew up in the same household or neighborhood. I had four sisters and five brothers. Most of the families in my 'hood were big and we still had our differences. Conversations were still like cross-culture communication. Women value evidence of connection when they are communicating. You want us to confirm we heard what you said because sometimes couples speak different gender dialects. Where women speak and hear the language of commitment and intimacy, men speak and hear language of sex and independence. Only then is the communication congruent with the desired outcome. Men and women will regard language from contrasting vantage points. The same story can be interpreted very differently. Learning and understanding the dynamics of male-female communication will make it easier to appreciate how dissatisfaction can be justified without blaming anyone or accusing someone else of being wrong.

Very often couples want to validate their commitment to each other by signing a promissory note to the union of holy matrimony – also known as a marriage license – but really don't want to relinquish all the vestiges of freedom. When men describe freedom as a benefit of divorce they are speaking of obligations to that person. They want to be less confined and are tired of being smothered, especially if it's causing deprivation of clout and popularity. Popularity is the main commodity that is bartered to obtain and maintain status. Bottom line, everyone wants to be heard and understood for what *they* think they're saying. Some men will talk about wanting to date in an open and honest way but are drawn or attracted to intrigue, mystery or challenge. There is something about not knowing everything about a person that is alluring. He doesn't necessarily need you to chase him, just show enough interest to keep him motivated. He wants to know you can love him with your head as well as your heart, and know you're not out chasing guys like a stalker.

Yes, you can flatter a shy man and tease the confident one, but don't chase him. I am not one to set a lot of rules, because it seems adolescent and contrived to give explicit instruction about guiding someone on the dating scene, unless they are very new at it. Know that every experience will be different and you'll learn from each one of them. Don't try to be a genius and be sure to guard your heart so you won't get your feelings hurt too often. I tend to adhere to my morals and then bend, stretch, break and make up rules for myself as I go along to avoid repeating previous mistakes.

Ladies, choose your conversations carefully. Remember to have fun in the beginning. Men really don't want to talk about things they don't know about or can't help you with. Some women, meanwhile, like to wallow in their problems with dialogue to a point of complaining either before or instead of trying a solution. Some of you become even more frustrated when the man doesn't show sensitivity, express interest or have patience to listen while you're ranting. Case in point: she crashed her car the week before, so she is driving his car until hers is repaired. She is driving home from work and the car stalls and she has to pull over on the side of the road. She calls her man and starts to rant: "Honey the car broke down, I'm on the side of the road and it's beginning to rain. Now, I am standing outside of the car for safety and this hussy just splashed water on my new dress, the one I brought from Saks. I have mud on my shoes and I have never been so humiliated in my life! I can't believe so many people drove by without offering to help me until this old man stopped by and offered a ride; I should be home soon. I was just wondering how I'm going to get to work tomorrow. I am just sooo upset!"

After the man learns that she's okay, he wants to know what is wrong with the car. He does not break in on the emotional rant because it would seem to show a lack of caring and sensitivity. But, in the back of his mind, he already knows she left the car on the side of the road and couldn't care less about the fate of it. He perceives this as a move by the woman to help her avoid confrontation. She was really pissed off at him for loaning her that piece of crap in the first place! It broke down on her! She knew he would get upset if she told him that, but she left the car on the side of the road... where it belongs.

The man will interpret what is between the lines of her ranting: she was trying to send a subliminal message rather than coming forward and being forthright. He may view the woman as a manipulative threat and her actions as sinister for refusing to clarify her message. It's not that the woman didn't want to get her point across or have her way; she just wanted to make her point without instigating an argument. This is what makes cultivating a relationship so unique and special, the fundamental difference in social structure between boys and girls, women and men. Ritual adversarial competitiveness is typical for a man and is displayed, or acted out, with rough play in games and sports. The aggression in a man is pervasive because it helps him with life challenges, struggles, competition, and it validates his self-esteem and status.

On the other hand, women are more challenged when trying to get their point across because men are more hard-headed and don't want to listen to women anyway. Therefore, women utilize their verbal skills when attempting to convey a message and find refuge in their display of class, awareness and style. One of women's most popular complaints is that men don't listen to them. However, you'll hear men make the same claim. But in actuality they both want to engage each other to ask questions, give advice, suggest options or make comments, favorable or otherwise. Women have a way of being so charming and engaging while communicating. You signal to men that you're following them in the conversation by saying *yeah, yes!, um-hmm* with quaint smiles and encouragements like you're in church helping the preacher deliver a sermon. Men will say yes only if they believe you or agree. Women are more inclined to be optimistic and see the sunny side of things and express just as much enthusiasm about a man's success as she does toward her own. Women aren't as intimidated by a man's success as a man is about a woman's success.

There's nothing quite as disarming, alluring and engaging as a good laugh. Telling jokes and making others laugh can give you power over them and temporarily disarm them in a fleeting, evanescent kind of way. You've heard of laughing your way to the bank? Well, you can laugh your way to bed as well. If you're confident enough, courageous enough and witty enough to become a positive, humorous reinforcement, you can influence and have your way with a man. If you can make a man laugh, it not only makes him temporarily happy, but it makes him glad to have you as a friend. This factor makes it easier to break down the walls of complexity. Of course, the man doesn't always want to be the butt of the joke. This kind of diversion can cause resentment or could be viewed as disparaging. By all means though, use humor as a motivating factor. We're suckers for a good joke or laugh and need them more than we know. Just pay attention to where the line of denigration is, and do your best to not cross it at his expense!

We should never be so proud and forthright that we can't be wrong, or admit we're wrong. It's hard to build trust in a relationship if we can't admit our mistakes. I think this is a part of what makes President Obama a believable person. He is not afraid to admit when he has screwed up. I can't remember the last time a president came forward with information about his mistakes... unless he was forced to do so. There is nothing like an apology and a counter-apology to balance things and keep both parties on the same page. I've seen cases where an apology is badly needed and two people aren't speaking to each other without it. It's the key to forgiveness. A simple apology could help avoid a fight or prevent going to war. The power is not always with the person who leads the household, or spearheads the idea; the power lies in the compromise.

Understanding the motives behind his interest in you is the first move in breaking a destructive current of communication. For an example, women and men have different needs for companionship which result in different behaviors. Women may have possessive sensitivities and a need for ownership whereas a man may have a desire for socializing and a need for independence. Now let the "games" begin. In the beginning, negotiations are of paramount importance. The man wants to appear trustworthy and promising, while the woman wants to hear if his story is good enough to tickle her fantasy. Could you be... her knight in shining armor? Go ahead and make her day.

A lady likes mental toughness, especially if it's in a down-to-earth kind of way. Bring it on. Show me what you're working with, whatever floats your boat, because she knows the water that is floating his boat may not be deep enough for her ship to sail all the way to shore! All the while in the man's mind, he understands the beauty of anticipation. He's thinking and singing to himself: *Oh when her ship... comes sailing in... oh when her ship... comes sailing in... I am going to feast on her fresh glazed donuts... oh, when her ship comes sailing in!*

Here's the irony, which also can be seen as the down side to cultivating a relation. Women are more socially expressive, descriptive and unrestrained when they're with their girlfriends, and the same can be said about men when they're with their fellas. Both men and women have to learn to be open and honest about what

they want from each other. Be up front in the beginning
to avoid the tumultuous rush to explain what may seem
to be the end of the relation. Women are talking about
the lack of good men, and the men are calling the
women gold-diggers. Women are using their bodies to
get what they want... and the men are using their toys to
get what they desire. Can't we just get along?

Yes, it's true, some women do have difficulty
finding a good man, because they are chasing after the
ten percent of the men who are successful, attractive,
and have the material things. Men are chasing the
roundest ass, the biggest tits or the cutest face they can
find with minimum focus on the woman's mental
capacity, emotional stability or her ability to be self-
sufficient. Both men and women are sorely misjudging
the core of what it takes to become the person they
would want to live with for the rest of their lives. I
know these things come with time, but the clock is
ticking the moment you meet. You may be looking for a
husband, baby-daddy or to be a baby's-momma and you
need someone to get serious with. Ladies you need to
step back a foot or two and observe whether he's your
kind of guy, the thoughtful type.

Here are a few good core traits of a man:
willingness to be patient, sensitive but strong,
dependable, willing to commit, supportive (the kind of
man who has your back in a crunch), good sense of
humor, and knows how to save money. Look for the
honest type you can trust, which means you won't have
to *try* to change much of him in the future. Now, if you
can also get a hot face and body bottled up with those

other characteristics, more power to you! These things and more are definitely on a man's mind, 'cause he wants fries with that shake when he's thinking about a woman of significance. They are the mantra for starting an everlasting relationship or marriage, raising children and grandkids, while growing gray together – or going bald together – with this lady, in love and happiness forever and ever.

Not to be overlooked is the singles sector, the single men who enjoy their status and privileges. Single men calculate how much time they can devote to their social lives. If the woman wants to get more serious about the relation before the man does, communication may be more challenging. A man has a number of fears if he's trying to impress a woman. He fears saying the wrong things, hurting her feelings or revealing a lack of knowledge on a subject. Then there may be a lack of finances, proper table manners or the lack of etiquette that may have him wondering if he has enough class. A real bachelor will find common ground if he's interested. He knows that a relationship can be negotiated and modified to fit the needs of the interested parties. You give and take, measure the pros and cons. Then, and only then, can this bond act as the foundation for the full challenge of the journey.

7

Honor His Integrity and Expect Him to Lie

Honor and trust perpetuates love

Most of the single guys I've talked to want to have their cake and eat it too. They tell me they want to "keep their options open" not because they want to date more women, but because it makes them feel they are in control of their lives. They say they want to enjoy the option of exercising their liberties. The majority of these men looked for faults or flaws in the women who tried to get too close. This may be a ploy to help obscure their irrational behavior, personal flaws and phobia about commitment.

The man is in charge of what he wants you to know and not know about him. Some men conceal information they know will hurt or anger you. It may be difficult to detect lies of omission when they fall silently into the spaces between spoken words. Some women don't want to discover or believe their man is lying or cheating. She may prefer to turn a blind eye. They don't want to take themselves through the horrendous pain, dreadful deception and irreparable betrayal. Lies can take root in your life and grow like poison ivy, putting safety and desirability at risk. A lie is a conscious behavior that is deliberate with the intent to deceive. These actions will invariably come back to bite you. What goes around comes around. But ladies, you might consider some men who just don't believe some of what they will tell you – or not tell you – actually represents a lie, per se. It may seem twisted from your perspective, but let me explain how some men work this out.

One of the biggest lies a man will ever tell you is, "I'll never lie to you." For that matter, the great enemy of the truth is very often not the lie, but rather and instead the myth, the innuendo, the accusations – because they are often persistent and pervasive. Love and suspicion seem so contradictory. But a man will often lie about his past to keep it behind him in an effort to let bygones be bygones. Like what happened in Vegas needs to stay there. So you must decide: How important is it to know the whole story anyway? You can't handle the truth! That's why there is so much *truth decay* in social behavior today. Keep in mind that I'm not referring to the inadvertent, misleading tales; the exaggerated promises, oversights and failures of communication. We can all appreciate the white lies we tell by over-exaggerating a bit of flattery in the interest of diplomacy. So let's be fair, not every man is a liar and not every liar is a man. Partners may want to discuss the boundaries of information they would be privy to share.

The real issue with men telling the complete truth is that the degree of punishment they'll likely receive is the same for getting caught in a lie. Therefore ladies, you have to give the man special consideration for telling the truth even if it causes you some disappointment. Otherwise, he'll feel it is better to lie and avoid the anguish of your disappointment. In reality, most of the lies men tell go undetected. It's probably just as well that they go unnoticed. I don't think it's healthy for any relationship to be put under constant scrutiny. I don't think it is fair for a woman to expect a man to give her every detail about his past. Don't look for him to give you all the details of what went on today or what he's thinking about for his immediate future or long term goals. We're just not big on itemizing specifics. Such explicitness could be considered as feminine or something a woman would do.

Many women make the mistake of thinking there's a direct correlation between making love, and love and fidelity. Consequently, it is like shutting off the brain because their heart is involved. There still isn't anything you can do to replace time as it relates to getting to know someone. Love is just as much a verb as it is a noun. It requires entities (a person or persons) and their actions. When you couple that with another person who possesses the same attraction and willingness to act upon mutual interest, usually that's how relations get started. Don't be fooled by the words "I love you."

Men are usually the aggressors when it comes to initiating the first contact. Therefore a man will volunteer himself as the promoter and entertainer of the beginning stages in relations. As a result, we'll exaggerate a little, or misrepresent the truth a little in the interest of keeping you engaged and wanting to hear more. Or perhaps exaggerate a lot in the interest of just getting in your panties. At that point, the pressure is on. All of a sudden we're on stage reaching for words to explain our deepest thoughts, ambitions and ultimate goals. Yet all the while we are holding back the thoughts of how sweet your glazed donuts are going to be. I'm wondering, "Who's idea was it to put a hole in the middle of the donut anyway?" all the while staying in sync with the conversation on the surface. Many men have untold passions that are dying to be heard, which shouldn't be considered honest or deceiving. I guess the best question for you ladies in this case would be, "Do you want to know about all of his passions, indiscretions and fantasies?"

I guess it is fair to say that some women like to be lied to, because they will lie to themselves about the lie. This type of woman might utter something like, "I know he wouldn't lie to me about something as simple as that"... whatever "that" may be. Even if her girlfriend spotted the man in a compromising situation, this type of woman would declare she has never given her man a reason to lie to her, intending to avoid the reality of deceit. What's most distressing about discovering a lie is having to live with it, topped off with having to live with him. Have you prepared yourself for handling a debilitating lie? It's better to be prepared for a lie and never hear it, as opposed to hearing a lie and not being prepared. The threat of *revenge sex* looms over both party's heads. But at the end of the day it comes down to value. How much do the two of you value each other? As I see it, everything can be negotiated. Don't be afraid of change, because there will always be many changing aspects within life. Changes being inevitable, you should direct them rather than simply continue to go through them.

If a man's fear of commitment is strong enough, he will ultimately sabotage, resist or run away from a relationship. There are men who value their independence so much that they are quick to notice when a friendship is starting to get "too serious." They tell me this is what takes all of the fun out of the relationship. The woman begins to ask for more time and becomes more demanding. The man begins to look for his parachute by withdrawing, provoking arguments and ignoring a woman's emotional needs. At this point, he has begun to run from you literally and figuratively. Sometimes it's the social style differences and other times it can be her insistence on constant communication that is too intense for him. Is it always the fault of the woman? No, it's not always the fault of the woman, just the fault of her judgment or interpretation of who the right man may be for her. Some women's need for "social security" can cloud their vision and block their ability to see a commitment-phobic man, causing her even more heartbreak and disappointment.

The man who cares about your feelings will tell you up front he's not looking for a wife or a serious commitment at this time in his life. That may be one of his most difficult decisions, depending on how he feels toward you. If he thinks he might want to keep you around and invest in your potential, he may not be so forthright about disclosing his unwillingness to commit.

When you meet a man and he tells you he's "just dating" right now, that doesn't mean things are going to change because he's dating *you*. Personally, I think a man should be clear about what he desires from a relationship and then give a lady updates as things change. I applaud talk-show host Michael Baisden for his effort in imploring men to stand up, be men, and arm women with the truth. If I could be the referee in your battle for affection, I would tell you, "keep your guard up, protect yourself at all times... and no hitting below the belt!" Now if the two of you decide to take the gloves off, there's a greater need to be honest. Here's the problem for men. If we tell you the truth we stand a chance of losing you, and if we get caught lying or cheating we stand the same chance of losing you. Most men take the chance on you not catching them. They would rather roll the dice on the chance that you'll never find out they're seeing someone else, as opposed to telling you they are seeing someone else, and losing you for sure. (This kind of conduct happens to be good for the goose.)

This takes me to the verge of compromise, because I believe a man should score points for honesty. If ladies continue to punish honesty, men will continue to lie. When it's so easy to tell a lie and much harder to tell the truth, what's our motivation to be truthful out of the gate? Give us freedom! I think it's an American thing with some men. It's in their nature. Men want women who are devoted to them and at the same time trust them enough to give them their freedom. And it doesn't really matter whether you think it's right or wrong. Men of all nationalities have fought for it. America has fought for it. "Let Freedom Ring," as the National Anthem says. That doesn't mean a man has to run off. Some just fall off the face of the earth and you never hear from them again. Some fly out of town like the Tasmanian Devil or like the old dapper cartoon cat, Snagglepuss: "Heavens to Murgatroyd! Exit, stage right." Ladies, I know, some of us men can take off so fast. Don't get me lying for them.

A man can sense when you're looking for love and will figure out ways to pause it. He knows that you like the shortness of breath with your heart beating fast, but ain't trying to cause-it. Maybe he's tired of fighting you off with his right hand while using his left to wrestle with all the things in his closet.

8

How to Learn a Man's Heart

His heart beats to the rhythm of his soul

The heart is the vital center of our being. It is the central, innermost control board for our emotions, feelings and devotions. Your heart gives you the capacity for sympathy, concern, compassion and love. It is the most important body part, the organ that facilitates willingness, mood, courage and affection, while the rhythmic pulsation of its beat drives our impulse. The heart is more than a notion and you shouldn't approach it as a notion. There's a lot to be said about the heart. The Bible says "God has planted eternity in the human heart." One day the beat of your heart will stop, ending your time on earth. Although life on earth offers many options and choices, eternity on the other hand only offers two: heaven or hell. This is the reason why it's so important to discover the desires of your own heart and use it wisely, for as it is written in the Good Book, "Thy will be done on earth, so that we may begin living in the light of eternity."

What are the matters of the heart? One involves the theory of longevity in a marriage. According to this theory, it is crucial to become friends first, to be selfless and to learn to compromise. Why do some couples stay married for 50 years and others don't make it to the fifth year? Some women say he had a change of heart, others may say he was heartless; or that he started off as a heartthrob but then had heart failure. What I've learned is this: there's nothing more important than making the time to get to know a person's heart. Ladies, you must study your man like Chinese arithmetic – even while using the utmost discretion to accomplish this studious undertaking. Watch the way he functions around other people: coworkers, employees, family, friends, his mechanic or fitness instructor, the cashier or the bank teller. Does he like children or animals? Is he patient, thoughtful or considerate of others' feelings? Does he have a quick temper? Is he good at saving money, does he have good credit, and what are his plans for the future? Does he lie to other people in your presence? Have you seen his sensitive side? Have you seen him mad as hell? Would he offer help to a perfect stranger? And does he always have a story to tell?

One of the biggest mistakes women make before committing to a man is not taking the time to learn his heart. Knowing his heart is having the ability to predict how he would handle a situation before it occurs; knowing what he would or would not do, even if he were accused of something outrageous, or of something entirely plausible!

Unified couples establish personal values, rather than relying on the values and expectations set by society. You have to decide whether a man holds the same appreciation for 'matters of the heart' as you. For example, two virtues that reign supreme in the mind of the kind of fella I like to call an *Idea Man* are wisdom and compassion. To this kind of man, the most valuable things in life are not *things* at all. Possessions only provide temporary happiness and are the reason most people wander through life with no deep knowledge or strong, authentic purpose. For this reason, the graveyard is the richest land in the world, because that's where all the unused potential, dreams, goals and aspirations are buried. The people who lived life with no direction, no meaning, and no sense of purpose took their values and valuables to their graves with them... turning it into a heart land. For some other people, the greatest disappointment was not in their death, but in their unfulfilled life... not knowing why they were here in the first place. It's very difficult to find a man's heart if he's not using it for anything. If a grown man hasn't found anything to wrap his heart around, he's probably not living a purpose-filled life, which can be considered a form of heart disease. I'll tell you what else is disheartening. Too many women are under the influence of a man's facade and may disregard his integrity without acknowledging their own ulterior motives for getting to know him. Ladies, I recommend you choose a new interest that you and your man can engage in together, something you can pursue jointly, be it chores, games, hobbies, charities, social activities or special projects.

Women have to be conscientious about how they evaluate the nature of a man – and I mean starting from the first handshake – if they want to avoid getting their heart broken. That's right, a touch is what I use to disarm my clients when they come to see me for the first time and they look a little nervous or apprehensive. I'll touch their neck or shoulders to help relax them and give off a warm and friendly impression. I've learned to study my clients' movements to better to assess their health and conditioning, taking note of their posture (which reveals age, class and mannerisms), as well as their tone of voice on the phone and in person. I try to determine their mood and their *modus operandi*. If she talks fast, I'll talk fast and if she talks slow, I'll talk slow. If you mix that up, you'll lose some of the intricate qualities of communication that can be heartfelt.

Can we talk heart to heart? Men play love to get sex and women play sex to get love. Sex is the magnet, romance is the journey... and if you don't call your preacher, I won't call my attorney. Our intuitive skills have us spotting and sizing up a potential mate from 100 feet away within two minutes; and it just takes mere seconds to decide if we find someone physically attractive. If a man knows he fits your ideal of an Adonis, he will overlook your economic or religious background to get right to your social values. It is usually lust at first sight and love in hindsight. One theory has it that the heart follows the beliefs of the man; therefore heroes, Average Joes and thugs have fundamentally different viewpoints. This means they would have dissimilar approaches to relations. Beliefs do matter, so your learning what he believes will help guide you to his heart.

One of the major issues with married couples is the lack of affection from partners. The sexual relationship can be what is most deeply satisfying and fulfilling in successful marriages but after an extended time together, some couples can sometimes forget to hang on to the simple expressions of affection – a kind or flattering word, a soft smile, a gentle touch to the shoulder or arm for reassurance and friendly physical reinforcement. What I'm trying to say is, if you believe his heart is willing and able to give you constant emotional and demonstrable physical affection – and not just the overt acts like pawing at you but also the gentle, subtle touches and gestures – then he may be marriage material. Of course, you have to be willing and able to demonstrate such polite, if "public" displays of affection toward him, too!

Sexuality is an open term that encompasses the set of beliefs, values, and behavior that defines each of us as sexual beings. Our sexuality is shaped by our upbringing, culture and religious beliefs. Some would say sex is the heartbeat of a relationship, giving new meaning to the notion of "hardening my heart." By no means am I suggesting that you seduce a man in search of his heart. Find it the old-fashioned way – take your time and learn it. Guys have a way of hiding their heart to keep you from breaking it. For us, the concepts of physical versus emotional sex can sometimes get a little distorted.

Coexisting is a key element of partnering, and the union of holy matrimony is another level of commitment in the context of partnering. As women are beginning to make equal or more money as compared to men, the rules of engagement are beginning to change. In a 1996 international Gallup poll, researchers surveyed residents of 22 countries. They found that women were perceived as being more affectionate, emotional, talkative and patient than men. Men were perceived across those 22 nations and cultures as being more aggressive, ambitious, and courageous than women. American society is moving away from male dominance to a more equitable gender role dynamic, thus many of the gender roles are getting based on who is the breadwinner in the family. In other words, as the world turns and the more contemporary our views are becoming, both sexes are capable and willing to successfully take on a variety of roles in the household. Meaning: both men and women are sharing a workable mix of masculinity and femininity; an androgynous relation, having both female and male characteristics. For example, there's the stay-at-home dad who cares for the kids (which gives new meaning to showing your feminine side), and the wife who repairs the car and cuts the grass. Despite the gender role stereotypes, men can be sensitive, patient and nurturing. It just depends on where his heart is. He might want to sleep with his fiancée before he marries her. I'd hate for him to find out that she was a hermaphrodite on the honeymoon or some such. This could cause a heart attack!

Seriously, despite the change in gender roles, women continue to not only multi-task – doing most of the housework, child-raising, and management of household systems and finances – but they also have to look on as men are becoming even less involved with household duties. Women refuse to go along with calling themselves nontraditional or feminist, but clearly they live more progressive lives than their mothers or grandmothers did in their time. Your reward should be that you can have any man you want. That's right. But the problem comes in when you don't know what kind of man you want and you settle for any kind of man who approaches you.

This became painfully obvious to me when I saw some women on an Oprah Winfrey show broadcast in 2009 listing more than forty different qualities they expect in a man. I was thinking, *Damn...I'm sure Jesus would get rejected if he were to approach some of these women!* Some successful women ask a lot of a man because they think they're qualified, and therefore privileged. However, any man who can uphold those standards is probably already very successful and may not be willing to cater to all of those needs. He'll be looking for someone to cherish him and his accomplishments and not necessarily expecting him to work so hard at it.

You will be better served to take a man who has very little and give him a taste of the good life. Turn his ass out. Steal his heart, put him under your spell and he'll love you forever, unconditionally. What really matters is whether *your* heart is in it or not. Your heart is the only timekeeper you'll hear and feel chiming inside your soul, with the speed adjusting to your motions and emotions. Your heart is your greatest mentor, coach and cheerleader. It will help you accomplish major tasks, while also giving you the intestinal fortitude to become all you can be. I see the heart as a precious learning tool I can trust. It won't let me down as often as my brain does. Have the heart to be who you are, even if it's not yet the *person* you want to be. Otherwise, you're just a fake. Have you ever wondered why some personalities stay popular with the public for long periods of time – Oprah, Ellen, Regis, Tyra, Jay, and David? Even radio personalities whom you can't see have staying power, like Donnie Simpson, Tom Joyner, Steve Harvey, Dick Clark, Casey Casem and Michael Baisden. They seem to keep a major following because they give it to you real and don't pretend. They give enough of themselves to allow us to learn their heart. The public accepts them as honest people, people you can listen to, people you can follow, people you can trust. It's really that simple in relationships, the love you give is the pleasure you get. The more real you are, the longer your legacy lasts.

If you want to look at how long David Letterman has been a big late-night star, you have to wonder how he even managed to withstand a scandal late in 2009 involving his ex-girlfriend, his wife, and a news producer at CBS (Dave's network), a scandal that eventually led to police charging the male news producer with attempted extortion! Dave is so popular that he was able to wisecrack about the episode even while folks were being marched off in handcuffs. All the while, a slew of female former show employees were turning up on CNN and everywhere else talking about how they had sex with him at work! I think Dave and these other celebrities stay popular, even in the midst of bad public relations-storms, because the public believes that they can recognize the *pure heart* of these individuals.

A man's heart changes as he grows older, so you have to listen to him with an attentive ear. Expose him to different things and situations to gauge his reactions. Observe his passions, make him mad, make him happy, check his responses. Watch the choices he makes and try not to define a man by some preconceived notions. Look at the way he treats his grandmother, mother, sisters and female relatives. Then turn the looking-glass to yourself: Are you equally yoked? Do you share some of the same physical, intellectual, emotional, spiritual and professional needs? Is he courteous to you? Can you get him to do things without nagging him? You will know how and when you are effectively learning his heart when you are able to get information out of him without asking any questions. When you can predict how he's going to react to a question or problem, good or bad news, or his favorite meal. When you've learned the recipes for his favorite cocktails, the cable channels showing his favorite pro sports contests, his type of movies, music, cars, clothing, style and taste, you are well on your way to seeing the shape of his heart piercing through the protective guards of his ribs. If you want him to love you with all of his heart – and if you want to avoid heartburn (which I suspect you do!) – remember: we're just ordinary people, we don't know which way to go... maybe you should take it slow.

Only a shallow woman would stay with a man for material things and money, knowing that he didn't have a heart. Most women are looking for a man with a loving, caring, compassionate heart; this is the glue that holds intimate relationships together. A man with a loving, caring and compassionate heart will do most anything to impress you, from breaking the rules to breaking the law to try and please you. Even sometimes by doing things that aren't very smart, a man like that allows you to take comfort in saying, *"He's a man after my own heart."*

9

The Insecurities of Men

Every man has a weakness in life

From the first moment a man decides that he wants you as his lady, his thoughts begin to cloud over with resentfulness. He is already worrying about any other man who might be of interest to you. Real or imagined, he is anticipating something that is common to most men at some point in their romantic lives: jealousy. It is a very powerful emotion, one that can eat into a man's insides like a cancer, until it guts him like a fish. Jealousy can make him half the man he should be. This green-eyed monster can take away some of a man's stability, leading him to feel out of control. This can happen when what he really, really wants is you... so, be careful, ladies. This emotional, knee-jerk response only intensifies after you turn his ass out!

At the same time, I believe that it is cool for guys to feel at least some jealousy at times. It helps to keep both of you on your toes within your relationship. Many people think it *proves* love, but it doesn't. Trying to make jealousy a litmus test for love could be very dangerous, as the two are not related. It may be more of a measure of one's insecurity or possessiveness than the depth of one's love. It is very important that you ladies monitor a man's jealousy and respect that there are various manifestations. A little jealousy will only confirm his desired affection for you and safeguard your exclusiveness. On the other hand, it can also spiral out of control and become irrational, destroying the relationship with its insistent unhealthy demands.

Both parties need to recognize when and how jealousy is useful and functional, and when and how it isn't. I've seen men act strangely as a result of jealousy, sometimes by reacting unreasonably toward other men, rolling on them with aggression and threatening violence.

What's even more haunting is the fact that your man could direct his jealous aggression *toward you*. Essentially, an insecure man must set boundaries for his relationship to minimize the negative fallout from his insecurities. This is vitally important, because others will only provoke him by trespassing his limits. A man feels psychologically less valuable, less attractive and less acceptable to his partner when he's overly jealous. This in turn only adds to his insecurities. It can be a vicious cycle. Jealous behavior can also be more intense for men in committed or marital relationships, where both parties have assumed the other's loyalty. With men, even if he's just dating you he will quite normally expect that you two are "exclusive." That doesn't necessarily mean he thinks *he's got to behave* like you two are exclusive, but he just wants to know that you treat it that way. (Yeah, it is a double-standard, but this is how many men think.) Therefore, the pain that he feels from jealousy is intertwined with his ego, propelling a greater sense of hurt, anger, deceit, agony, doubt and depression. For these reasons, men are apprehensive about revealing their vulnerable side. They can be reluctant to confide in and trust a woman with whom they are in a committed, loving relationship. As the relationship becomes more and more intimate we become less and less independent.

For some men, the increase of interdependence will only heighten the fear of losing his love interest. Not by any means am I trying to suggest that dependency is a major cause for jealousy, but rather, it is his fear that the loyalty he feels for you will be violated should you cheat. The thought of you engaging in infidelity and unfaithfulness can trigger him to lose his mind... especially *if* he's been faithful. It takes very little to provoke an insecure man: talking to another man too long in his presence, showing kind gestures, making a lingering touch or, God forbid, you lock eyes with another man too long. A man has natural insecurities about his partner's attraction to someone else.

Sometimes a little jealousy is a good way to measure how a man will react to adversity, genuine threats, misleading perceptions or interpretations, and suspicions. If your man displays signs that he is jealous, it can be a good time for you to observe how he thinks and reacts to his insecurities and inadequacies. But make no mistake, these feelings lay within the man, not within the relationship. An excessively jealous man will need lots of reassurance and, as a result, he could attempt to emotionally imprison you with his insecurities. Some psychologists suggest that men are more jealous in cases of physical infidelity than in cases of emotional infidelity. Women, on the other hand, are more likely to become more jealous in cases of emotional infidelity than in cases of sexual infidelity. The man's concern about his partner's infidelity is rooted, at least in part, in his concerns that any child that you have "together" may not be his! But the woman isn't as concerned about whose child it is. She is more concerned about his protection and support while child rearing. Thus, emotional attachment between the two of you is crucial. A woman may believe her man is capable of having sex without being in love; however, a man may believe his woman is falling in love with another man if she cheats on him. A man feels that a woman will only have sex with a man she's falling in love with.

The manner in which social, environmental, biological and evolutionary factors may underlie gender differences is a highly controversial question that remains unanswered. One of the greatest psychoanalysts of all time, Sigmund Freud, once said, "A human being is a resultant of constitution and fate, or heredity and environment."

Often times there can be a legitimate reason for jealousy, such as when there's a third party involved who may violate the boundaries of the relationship. To avoid a relationship crisis, communication and recognition of the feelings of all parties involved must be honored and respected. Understanding and agreed-upon appreciation for the relationship can then be restored.

We all sometimes have mood swings, though I believe they are more common for women than men. Mood changes are a normal part of everyday life. At times we feel sad, upset or depressed. But be careful of extremely "down" or "up" moods that linger on, and are so profound that they affect your ability to function rationally. They could be life threatening, causing the man to lose touch with reality. This behavior could represent a mood disorder, and it is important to recognize emerging signs of this in yourself, or in your partner. Although researchers say depression occurs twice as often in women as it does men, I would caution women about social depression in men. When a man spends countless hours and dollars pursing fruitless, ever-elusive, unattainable goals in efforts to win you as his lady, depression can set in if he discovers that you were just playing him all along.

It is a recognized feature in the behavior of paranoiacs that they place the greatest significance on trivial details that might be overlooked by others. A superstitious guy believes that peculiar occurrences will have an effect on shaping your future together without recognizing or accounting for his own contributing actions. Some guys experience anxiety in situations in which there's no external cause or reason for distress. He may experience feelings of envy or jealousy and could be suffering from a psychological disorder or inferiority complex which in turn could give you reason enough to change your social involvement with him.

An insecure man will use anger to help boost his feeling of strength, power and encouragement. Some use alcohol to develop confidence, which then perpetuates their anger and causes them to want to just go on and on arguing their point. Consequently, anger causes the man to substitute his feelings of superiority for those of rejection, hurt and disappointment. Both love and anger are intense emotional feelings with psychological components. This is why police officers know that domestic calls are among the most dangerous and unpredictable service calls they face. A man will fight for his freedom and independence the same as he'll fight for your loyalty and commitment; anything interfering with that will cause insecurity or jealousy. Sometimes a man has to be handled with finesse, and ladies have to employ a careful strategy to rid him of his funk, or suspicion. As the legendary 20th century philosopher, Reinhold Niebuhr, once wrote: "Father, give us courage to change what must be altered, serenity to accept what cannot be helped, and the insight to know one from the other."

One important set of characteristics common to a stable relationship is the couple's ability to be kind, courteous, thoughtful, nice and giving to one another. The ratio of positive to negative experiences should be at least four-to-one. By focusing on the positive, memorable moments of joy and laughter, and the times of passion and affection, you should be able to overcome the tough times of pain and anguish. Preserve your relationship by avoiding unnecessary conflict. Don't chase him into silent mode. Very often, men have problems facing the obstacles of a relationship and the dominant styles of some women. From my observation, some men are ambivalent about how to approach their relationship problems, and are insecure about whether to face head-on, or distance themselves from the chaos that they envision will follow. For that reason, a man will ponder again and again what is the correct cadence for the tone of voice that he will use to speak with you as he considers delivering his message and presenting his concerns. He will be careful not to disturb the delicate balance by overstepping the thin line between love and hate. Men wrestle with insecurities as they relate to dating, friendship and marriage. Also, always at the forefront of his mind is money, communication, time, family, chores... then whatever the soap opera of the day is.

A man's greatest insecurity usually concerns his financial position. Researchers have discovered that marital separation, divorce, domestic violence, drug and alcohol abuse are more likely the "poor man's problem," than for men in any other socioeconomic group. When the well-being of the family is secured financially, couples tend to focus on a more fulfilling relationship and a better quality of life. Still, don't get me wrong – money can't buy you love, it can just make it easier to find. I can tell you one thing that would make a man feel more secure about himself, and may also help keep that green-eyed monster away: having a partner who is careful and considerate with spending and saving money. While he is trying to survive in this stressful economy, a man needs to feel good about himself. Many are willing to learn new skills or trades to meet the challenges.

A man has every reason in the world to feel the pressures of life more acutely, perhaps, than a woman, because the buck stops with him. However, couples who compromise and share financial decisions are likely to have the least conflicts. To a certain degree, the partner with the most money, financial leverage and earning potential, has the most power or influence in the relationship. Not saying that's the way it *should* be, only that this is usually how it is!

As the great Al Green sang, "Let's Stay Together." I dare say that most people have a natural instinct to blame others and to avoid taking responsibility for their part in any problems that may emerge in a relationship. But it might help if we all try to remember that our mannerisms and communication styles change when we're under stress. For example, the pursuer may want to get closer to you if he thinks you aren't hearing him, while you may just want to get farther away in that moment, to keep sparks from flying. At those times, you want to try your best to not attack your partner's character or personality with criticism and contempt. And if an argument does ensue, both of you should attempt to keep it healthy, so that the both of you are able to recuperate from it.

Edit the information in the argument by only responding to constructive criticism and ignore any nasty inflammatory rhetoric. (And of course both of you should seek to avoid making any such nasty or inflammatory comments but, yeah, I know how it can go in the heat of battle!) Take a timeout, chill, or cool off before you try to make your point. Keep the fight in perspective, and you'll eventually find that the issues at hand probably weren't all that important anyway! Be fair and honest, understanding, empathetic and willing to compromise. Furthermore, if you can find it in your heart, try to laugh at the problem and find humor in the conflict. Own your own feelings and emotions, negotiate your wishes, focus on the issues at hand and always bring closure with a mutual agreement to respect each other. No sucker punching, hitting below the belt, or leaving imprints from a bite, 'cause love should be able to survive a fair fight.

There are a plethora of insecurities men ponder each and every day in their subconscious mind. Men want to be right all the time, even when we're driving – well, especially when we're driving. We won't ask for directions! Some men show instant discomfort when they are introduced to a new environment, a new conversation, a new perspective, or a new hottie. He's wondering, *Am I too short, too fat, too dumb? How's my breath? What does she really want from me?* The irony of it all is that the man who is most qualified and compatible for the woman is usually the one who questions his fortunes and prospects... while the man who has the least to offer the relation is usually the one who will pursue you with confidence! Ladies, it is almost like having a brand-new, expensive car. Your friends with money who have their own cars will never ask you if they can borrow your car. But a family member or friend who has no insurance and can't pay to replace the cigarette lighter, let alone pay for their own ride, is always asking for your keys! And a lot of the time, they have the nerve to be demanding it, like you're supposed to KNOW to just hand over the car keys!

Consider my cousin Rocky. He is 54, single, and has his own house and a good job. He is a nice-looking gentleman, too. I once asked him about his insecurities while we were talking about his concerns with growing old. He was saying how he doesn't currently have a Special Someone, and how he wonders if he'll ever find the woman he deserves. So I told Cousin Rocky the same thing that I'm going to tell you ladies here and now. We all deserve to meet our soul mate. Forrest Gump put it more plainly: Life is like a box of chocolates, you never know what you're going to get. Well, that box of chocolates has changed quite a bit over the past decades. And if you pick the right one, it just may turn out to become president of the United States! And picking the wrong one means you certainly better learn to be cognizant of his insecurities.

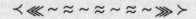

10

A Man's Subconscious Thoughts

What he's really thinking (but not telling you)

When he is making decisions about a woman, a man's actions are always in danger of getting in the way of his thought processes. By this I mean: On some of those occasions when he is hanging with you, going to the movies or to lunch, he may be there with you in "real time," but subconsciously he is at the game with his boys.

Men spend an overwhelming amount of time thinking about and planning out, in their minds, the way they see things – only to later discover that you had a better idea. Just know this: a man who is really attracted to you will be thinking in mysterious ways about how he can impress you. The man wonders how he can get the most out of life, but is also thinking about the degree of sacrifice he'll have to make to achieve the life he envisions with you. He wants to live in faith that the whole world is on his side. He's thinking, "Should I get married and have children, or should I stay single and be more ambitious career-wise... or can I do both?" And because actions have a way of getting in the way of a man's thoughts, he ends up with a baby and finds himself proclaiming that he didn't plan it – but that he's happy he had it. Riiiiight! His decision-making abilities were clouded well before that point. More men have used this consequential approach to their destinies than the well-planned out approach, which is why there are so many missing fathers, and good men handcuffed to bad decisions. In their minds, guys are running and running from obligations they cannot dream of handling.

Men have to realize that our destiny is shaped by the choices we make today! And few choices are more important than how, why or when we penetrate a woman. We can't be absolutely sure you're on birth control. He can't tell if he's sleeping with the enemy. Some guys consider themselves quick-draw withdraw, and some ladies like to ride the horse without a saddle – to protect or not to protect.

I've often wished that I could wake up the next morning and push a reset button to have everything go back to the way it was before I went to bed. But then I realized that the reset button was safely protected inside the confines of my thick skull. Men do a lot of begging for forgiveness because we have so many distractions and opportunities that require a clear head. It can be damn confusing when we have blood rushing to one of our "heads." The other head (the one on our shoulders!) seems to lose all sensibilities when this happens and is influenced by what it has discovered as a development. All the while, we're thinking...

"I'm not sure how much of my freedom I'll have to give up by securing your loyalty."

The man assesses how he's doing personally before making a decision about how much time he can devote to a relationship. As in: "Let's see. I can afford to pay the mortgage, I have a decent car...decently dressed! Got a solid job, things are going well for me. I think I'll stay single for now." On the other hand, if things aren't going so well and he thinks he might need some support in the near future, he may have more interest in "qualifying you" for an opportunity to move in together. At that point, freedom isn't as important to him as securing your loyalty. Otherwise, gaining trust is a long-term thing. Don't take for granted that because a man commits to living with you, he's totally into you. Do your homework about the man's true motivation for agreeing to cohabit.

"The more you push your availability on me, the less I want to see you."

As the saying goes, he won't miss his water until the well runs dry. Relations last longer when you don't see each other as often, at least in the early stages of your romance. Take the time to savor the relationship and indulge the precious moments. You never know how long they are going to last. People invest exorbitant amounts of time preparing for the success of the relationship and make very little preparation for its failure. This makes it harder to bring closure to a relation that has not worked out. Closure may come in many colors. Just accept it and move on. Now if it's just a matter of availability or lack of time, two people can usually work things out. But if it's a matter of which day or what time to have sex, it's probably better to allow the man to decide. After all, he's Clark Kent waiting on an opportunity to be Superman! The man is the one who has to transform his body part to perform or please a lady, so it seems to me that his vantage point would be more important in this regard.

"I chose a lady who I think is smarter and has more potential than me, but I resent her 'lording' it over me."

The magic of thinking big means to *date potential*. Be open-minded enough to spot a man who has potential and a bright future regardless of the level he currently occupies. Michelle Obama dated potential and overlooked the old, beat-up car that her date, a young lawyer named Barack Obama, was driving. It had holes in the floor and was a sorry hoopty indeed. Michelle concentrated on the content of his character, his ambition and his caring ways. She saw a sparkling future in him, even if she had to squint her eyes to catch a glimpse of it! Men are more willing to invest in potential and see themselves as the breadwinner. Women have to look beneath the surface and find their real-life hero, and then resist reminding him of their investment in his earlier, hoopty version. If the woman is a lawyer and the man is a janitor then she shouldn't automatically disregard his opinions or perceived level of intelligence just because he's not a professional in this area. The moral is that you don't have to be a learned person to be a wise person.

"I want you to take care of me, but not exercise the control that comes with that."

No matter how down-and-out a man might appear to be, he still wants to be in on the decisions being made that involve the two of you. The last thing a man wants is a boss in the house when he gets home. Is it too much to ask of you to act like you're happy to see him when he comes home – and to let him have the big piece of chicken? A man simply wants to feel important.

"I feel important when I take care of you, but I also expect you to take care of yourself."

It seems like a man's goal in life is to take care of a woman. The most significant role long associated with "manhood" was the macho job he held as protector and chief. The man was supposed to earn a living and provide food and shelter for his family. My, my, my, how times have changed. Contemporary women could very well be the breadwinner with the larger income now and in some cases, the single parent of the household. Men respect and understand the potential of women, and especially with economic times being as hard has they are currently, sometimes it does take two to make a household run smoothly. Nobody is getting a free ride these days and as the world turns, the financial wave of currency can change at any moment for any given situation. Can somebody say liberation!

"I fear exposing my vulnerability to the relationship because it means my weaknesses will be revealed."

"We are vulnerable both by water and land, without either fleet or army," wrote Alexander Hamilton, one of America's founding fathers. Men yield their vulnerable side when they're overcome with emotions, which weakens their ability to make good, strong decisions. This leaves them inclined to giving in to persuasion or temptation, which in turn makes them susceptible to attack... or to the sly moves of a lady. Real men have always prided themselves on being the strong, fearless leader of, and provider for, their flock. Therefore, many men consider any display of vulnerability as showing a "feminine side." I am not saying their jumping to this conclusion is realistic, or necessarily a real problem from the woman's point of view. I am just letting you know that many men equate showing any kind of vulnerability with being "weak" and that from there, they do the math and come up with "feminine."

"I feel empowered by your emotions, although I complain about them."

As a woman enlists the support of a man, she also empowers him and encourages him to "be all that he can be." A man feels empowered when he's appreciated; needed or trusted without the woman trying to change him. When a man listens to a woman's feelings and emotions without getting uptight or frustrated, this can be empowering to the woman. It makes her feel understood, accepted and free to express herself. And as long as this freedom doesn't parlay into a whine or a nag, there should be no reason for a man to complain.

"I know I only want you for sex... but I won't admit to it."

Can we be *friends with benefits*? This is a relatively new term, coined by teenagers and young adults in the 21st century to mean an efficient way of fulfilling sexual desires in our fast-paced world with a minimum of tiptoeing around or time-wasting. It is really just a handy way of describing friends who have a sexual relationship without any emotional commitment. Essentially, they consider themselves friends, with no intentions of having a monogamous boyfriend-girlfriend type of commitment and without any strings attached. They enjoy sex for the pleasures of it and, unlike casual sex that takes place between strangers, *friends with benefits* are familiar with each other and comfortable too, which makes them feel a sense of safety and convenience. I'm sure some of you may find this notion repulsive, while some will view it as a natural, healthy expression of sexuality. The question is not whether it's right or wrong, but rather, why is *friends with benefits* becoming more popular? Who's zooming who? Someone is getting rewards. Someone is having a lot of fun. Someone is knocking at the door, somebody is ringing my bell, must be a friend... do me a favor... let 'em in.

"I know you are the one for me. I like the way you make me feel when you're around."

Chemistry has a lot to do with the possibility that you may discover a *feel-good friend:* someone who makes you feel just like the person you are. You'll know when this happens because your approach and interactions will be as effortless as your support. A man really doesn't know what he wants from a particular woman until he meets her, and usually around the same time he discovers what she needs from him as well. Men are visceral creatures like that. You know the saying: You can make a monkey do anything if you have enough bananas. Well, ladies can get a man to do most anything if you can fulfill at least some of his wants and needs while indicating the promise of future delights. Throw him a banana, be it of the sexual, culinary, or visually-stimulating variety. You can get your man to jump through all kinds of hoops if you satisfy his wants and needs. Don't expect any special tricks if you run out of bananas. He's just going to jump through your hoop, the hoop he's already familiar with. At the same time, maybe you should view this as reciprocal metaphor, one in which he throws some bananas back at you. The moral of the story is to never under estimate a *feel-good friend.*

"I just don't know enough to broaden my conversation with your family and friends."

I can hang with discussing politics now that Obama is in the White House, but when the conversation swings to Wall Street I'm stumped. Look, I'll hang with your family as long as my lack of knowledge doesn't become their entertainment. And by contrast, it seems they never want to talk about sports, music, crime, poverty, or the police, all topics I know about. Oh honey, the things I'll do for you! A man will do most anything to please you, but may not be so enthusiastic about pleasing your family and friends.

"Even though I act tough and strong, I need love just like you and I'm just as confused about finding it."

If I could just figure out what love is. There are so many definitions of love. I'm not sure what kind of love I want or can give. Will love make me weak, vulnerable and lessen my focus? Am I in love with myself and really just need someone to reflect or project my ego? Am I in love with the thought or idea of being in love? Would that be narcissistic love? How do I know what love is? It is confusing. I know I prefer romantic and sexual love the best; however, I also will settle for a conscious love or a friendly one. That said, where do I begin to look? In the past, as the old R&B song says, "I've found love on a two way street and lost it on a lonely highway." Is love a myth or delusion, or whatever two people think it is? What really frightens me is the thin line between the ecstasy of salvation and the pitfalls of despair. There is no real guarantee that love from your partner will always be there.

"If it is quick and easy for me to say I love you, it will be quick and easy for me to leave you."

Some men play with the word love. It has a way of relaxing the woman, like tuning the radio to her favorite station. She begins to focus on the music and not the deejay. Ladies keep your focus on the messenger, for he's the one using the most powerful word in the English language: L-O-V-E. But when you put those letters together it should mean something special. Some men will use it as a protocol to get your panties on the floor, win your trust, get your house or car keys and much, much more. People define love according to their experiences, upbringing and background. Some see it as a way of acting with someone, a strong feeling, a way of treating or caring for someone else. All is fair in love. What's not fair is to use the thoughts of love as leverage to get your way with a person.

"If I fall too deeply in love with you that would limit my ability to protect myself from you."

Ladies, love is like Kryptonite to Superman. Even though it makes us weak and vulnerable, we become dependent on it and fall more in love with the person who's fulfilling our needs. That sounds good to you, doesn't it? But it is too bad you have to put a spell on a man to get him to act right. If you want to impress me, put a spell on me without the Kryptonite! What are you afraid of? Come on, you say you want a strong man who can protect you, take care of you and make you feel secure. But then you want to weaken him like a chaser in a nice glass of whiskey. You don't want him to be too strong or he just might get inebriated (drunk on himself). Come on ladies play fair... no cheating. If I *fall* in love with you, I don't want it to be because you pushed me. I want to be your hero, your Mandingo warrior, the only one you run to, the guy you trust to save you and only you. I'm here to tell you that I'm going to need my *balls* for that, so give them back and let me be the man you want.

"I don't want you to fall in love with me. It might change things for the worse."

When couples reach a point at which they totally understand and appreciate each other completely, and feel like they know one other, eventually they stop sharing new experiences with each other. This is what makes the passion fade. Then there's the physical and emotional arousal involved, which can become inconsistent when taken for granted, just making it easy for the cleanup woman. This is why cheating and secret sex is so intense; the person cheating experiences greater excitement. Romance is the way to keep things from changing for the worse. Keep changing your sexual presentation, offer something new and different. Show your sexy side when you're in the mood, be a romantic chameleon. Keep him guessing and you'll keep him horny. That's just what men love... the anticipation of something new. When one in the relationship falls in love, it changes the personality of the communications from fun to serious. What happened to the in-between stages? Can we go-there, and stay for a while please?

"I'm not sure I can completely satisfy you."

She wants a man who is sexy, smart, wealthy, strong, vulnerable, thoughtful, gentle, clever, attractive, honest, tall, genuine, considerate, and totally infatuated and in love with her. Damn, as good as she makes me feel I should be willing to do most anything and everything to keep her happy. Well, that's just about what it would take... everything, all of my time and most of my money. But eventually, the man is going to think: "How long can I hold up? When will I disappoint her? Can she be satisfied with me?" There's nothing more demoralizing than the feeling of not being qualified to maintain the interest of a desired attraction. Our ego gets in a fight with our conscience, but then eventually reality sets in, bringing us to conclude that maybe we'll just be your maintenance man (Mr. Right Now) until you find that dude (Mr. Right)!

"As much as I like strong women, I like them more when they agree with me."

Some people have a need to be in control while some others seem to avoid it. Understanding the difference in desire for power amongst couples and the motivation behind it will certainly take the edge off communications. Power can be as simple as influencing someone to get your way, or it can be as hard as making decisions that affect how your family lives. I believe in cohesive power but I also believe that expert power should rule. The person with more skills, superior knowledge or the most experience should be the one who has first choice or who acts as the authority in the matter. This is the way to exercise informational power without using too much psychological power. Deeper still, there's an application of power that rests on a thorough process. It goes like this. The one who possesses organizational power (the ability to envision and arrange systems or events) and/or implementing power (the ability to put in place the vision or event) will usually also then possess the bargaining power that is needed to plan the event or vision a success. This individual could be you, or it could be the man you are dating. Power to the people! What is most important is the ability to balance the power between you two. Laugh at his jokes even if they're not funny, stroke his ego every now and then, and let him be right once in a while (said with a smile).

"I see her power and control over the relationship as a sign of my weakness."

As we know, communication is key. It is the lifeblood of any relationship. Feeling powerless often derives from the lack of freedom to express one's abilities, knowledge and thoughts. An involved man wants to interject and contribute to the relation. It's supposed to be a man's world for-real-doh! We need your support, crave your approval and want to impress you. We want you to feel just as enthusiastic about our success as you feel about your own.

Unspoken

The revelations of a man's thoughts have fallen between the spaces of the words that he presents. When he's not ready, a man's thoughts are smothered by his lack of ambition when it comes to securing a woman's aspirations to be in a marital relationship.

As powerful as the unspoken word is, a woman's awareness is as weak.

Men are carrying thoughts around with them that they haven't begun to imagine. It's equated to the enormous amount of pressure he endures to secure your confidence in him. However, a real man is the master of his own fate and the supervisor of his soul. The things that are deep in the back of his mind are not always the things that you're told.

11

The Sexual Behavior of Man

One of the most powerful forces on earth

A man's sexual behavior is a complex combination of instinct and inheritance (cultural, social and biological). Some men say sex is one of the most powerful forces on earth. The magic seems to happen for just a few seconds, for *all that it's worth*.

This is how I imagine history unfolding. The physical urge to have sex was and remains an innate impulse, a programmed response, a basic instinct. After all, it was the only way to ensure the continuation of one's genetic line, one's race. Sex equaled long-term survival. The sexual behavior of men was very diverse and as a result gave rise to a wide spectrum of beliefs, customs and rituals. His sole purpose for engaging in sex was for reproduction, but like everything else, men turned it into an art form. They began to use their *penis power* for pleasure, especially when their partners made it a plum pleasing privilege. Men soon mastered the power of feeling good, which eventually meant that they didn't always obey the rules of morality. Nevertheless, because he was learning to cultivate his feelings and freedom of expression, he never thought more or less of his mate by addressing her as a Floozy or a Jezebel, neither did he consider her his Princess or Queen. It was just *sex in the village.*

Man's sexual behavior came to include oral sex, then anal sex, and wouldn't you know, it didn't take long before he stopped caring where he stuck it. Soon a man would brandish an arousal that never left the confines of his slippery grip of masturbation. I tell you, it was bad back in the day; men start shooting themselves off like it was their rifle. No, seriously, if you want behavior, I'll give you behavior! They knew they couldn't make babies like that.

Next came sexual entertainment and fantasies, fixations and fetishes, as well as philosophies and values prohibiting certain sexual activities and making much of them off limits to minors. I mention all that to say... hetero or homo, mutual or solo, incestuous or abusive, families have always had some issues with and about male sexuality, so don't act like it's just me. The ability to differentiate the innate biological tendencies from the cultural values, particulars of upbringing and earlier experiences is helpful in evaluating the sexual behavior of men.

A man's sexual experience encompasses more than just what we do, it is ongoing and evolving, a changing journey that incorporates delightful confluences of the body's meaningful emotions; an experience that will allow a man to use all of his senses to get him to a point where he receives a reward or a prize, compensation for his efforts. What's so fascinating is the signals our bodies send, and the way our senses help guide us into sexual action. Our senses (which are attached to our nerve endings) send signals to the brain. The brain sends a message to the heart to pump more blood to our penis... which begins to swell like an inflatable balloon. This gives the man the tool needed to make a baby, another life, another living example of God's most precious creation. "Power to the penis!"

When a man is holding his erection, it's almost like he's holding his whole world in this hand. He can do so many good or bad things with it! And when he plugs it into a willing woman's nucleus, he will for a *short* period render her speechless or influence her to become more vulnerable and maybe even fall in love with him. But on the other hand, he might place it in the wrong hole and turn his life upside down! Man, the trouble we can get into in the name of serving our sexual needs. Not surprisingly then, one of the safest choices is pleasuring ourselves. I see a lot of guys today struggling like mad because they just didn't know when or how to manage their sexual behavior. Some of these men you'll find in jail, some are working two or three jobs and some you'll see picking trash up along the roadside as you drive by, while some are just missing in action, prompting you to wonder why. Some men will try to sexualize anything and everything they see if it is wearing silk or lace. Some elderly men will tell you a hard-on is a terrible thing to waste. Sex can represent our highest human values of intense emotional contact, expressing true eroticism and reverence for life, while exploring the sensitivities of your heart and soul.

Nothing can compare to a woman's expressions while she's in the throes of ecstasy. It seems like the more animated she is and the more passion she releases, the manlier we men become. It's certainly a good way to prolong the erection. The more you ladies yell, the harder it swells. A man can easily lose an erection when his mind wanders on to something else. This is a natural occurrence, so don't be offended. Sometimes he needs you to get him in sync and keep him in focus with the pleasure is at hand. He needs you to help him drop the pressures of his day.

A man's sexual recipes help guide him to decide how creative he wants to be, based on his appetite. Sometimes when he calls you it's because he has a taste for you. Other times he may need a little encouragement. But don't continue to let him have his way without pleasing you first. Trust me, he always has room for dessert, aka, your fresh glazed donut. Sexual intercourse or the Latin word, *coitus,* involves a sense of sharing, and equal participation by both partners. Although men tend to experience orgasms more often than women, sexual pleasure is only one reason why men seek to have sex. If the woman wants to be more orgasmic, she'll have to teach her partner how to properly stimulate her clitoris before and during intercourse. Be aware of the untrained, over-hyped, impatient guys, the kind who make the mistake of handling the clitoris like it's a small penis, squeezing and grabbing it, applying too much pressure. Oh, and make sure he washes his hands first and tell him not to rub up against it with a stubby beard!

Some men need to be taught sexual adequacy. They need to learn about indirect touching, how to lightly graze their finger over the top, stroke the sides and lightly circle the clitoris with the tip of their finger and tongue. A man needs to know how to use the light warm wet moisture from his pulsating tongue, ever so gently caressing with warmth from his breath, while vibrating the clit with a low sound like a hummmmm... if you want him to make you cum. A man won't learn these things from watching videos or talking to the boys. Don't be afraid to tell him about your sensitive spots. Sometimes you just have to define your needs in a suggestive way. Some men think that all they have to do to help a woman reach orgasm is to pack the walls of her vagina and hit her highly sensitive spots, again and again. However, a great number of women need clitoral stimulation at the same time they are receiving the thrusting in and out movement. Let him know he may use a variety of touches in the beginning stages of stimulation, including using his hands and mouth, but when or if he finally gets your fuse lit... he'll have to stay consistent until you explode! It should be understood that some of you need manual stimulation during intercourse to be orgasmic. Therefore, women should not be at all shy about manually stimulating yourselves or by being stimulated by your mate before, during, and maybe after. I often wondered why the clitoris is positioned so high in the vulva anyway. I guess we'll just have to move our bodies upward to keep in constant contact with it for more stimulating pleasures. We can look at it this way, it's the one time a man can *screw-up* with his woman and get it right!

The first component of increasing your sexual pleasure is having your conditions met. Much of our sexual communications are nonverbal, indirect and ambiguous, and for those reasons they run a high risk of misinterpretation. Men often believe that women say no when they actually mean not now, coax me, get more creative or try harder. A man is more likely to flirt with a sexual purpose and interprets a woman's flirt as teasing. In addition to talking openly about contraception and safe sex, couples should communicate what they like and need sexually, such as which kind of foreplay or after-play each prefers. "How do you like your stimulation, honey? Manually or orally? Before, after or during?" "What will it take to make you orgasmic?" As we respect the power of nonverbal cues, let's not lose the pleasures of intimacy and compassion to ambiguity. One of a woman's most enduring challenges is keeping her man from feeling he's missing out on something in the relationship, keeping him sexually motivated so that he is never bored within a monogamous commitment.

A man's sexual dysfunctions include premature orgasm, lack of desire and erectile dysfunction. The fear of failure is the immediate cause of erectile dysfunction. Men experience performance anxiety when the sex-demanding woman chooses when and where to have intercourse. Though a man finds it difficult to say no to sex, he has to coordinate his mind, emotions and bodily functions. Therefore, ladies would be better served to let the man choose when the time is right for coitus. A woman's sexual dysfunctions are usually lack of desire, lack of orgasm, difficulty lubricating or having sex that is not pleasurable.

The first oral treatment for male impotence was Viagra, approved by the U.S. Food and Drug Administration in 1998. It became an economic and cultural phenomenon with sales of $1 billion the first year. By 2003, Levitra was approved for older men who had cardiovascular and other medical risks, and then Cialis was introduced to give longer effectiveness, its effects lasting up to 36 hours; this pill is known as the *weekend drug* and in some cases, if the sexual responsiveness improves, so does the relationship. Now granddad is out there getting his groove on making babies. That's why you see a lot of elderly men working now, because they've spent all their retirement money on young girls, chasing them around trying to *drive a hard bargain*!

Unintended pregnancy is one of the biggest setbacks for a man. He wakes up one day to find that he has a 20-year commitment to someone he hasn't even met. He's not sure if he wants to run, be happy or beg for forgiveness. An estimated four in ten American women become pregnant before they reach their twentieth birthday. This turns young men into cowards, creates dysfunctional families and is one of the major reasons why there's so much violence in the streets today amongst the youth. Babies are raising babies, mothers are working two jobs and men are taking side jobs to avoid paying taxes and child support.

Now, more than ever, there's a need for sexual responsibility, sexual literacy, disclosure of intentions and understanding what the purpose of sex is in your life. Each person should consciously develop a sexual philosophy. Do we need sex for intimacy, an exchange of passion, erotic pleasures, reproduction, developing love or other purposes? Partners should mutually agree upon sexual activities and keep it safe for both.

Experts estimate that at least 10 percent of American men are gay, and this sector is growing prouder every day. I've started to notice men walking around the Atlanta hair show wearing 5-6 inch heels and stretch pants, some with bald heads and some with hair down their backs. It seems Madea has been around so long her grandsons have gone to Morehouse College, causing professors to have serious problems keeping the students focused in the classrooms. Men are coming to class out-dressing the women; wearing makeup, miniskirts, stilettos; carrying purses and wearing wigs and weaves. I'm not saying a guy shouldn't express himself, though I do have a problem with the appropriateness of his actions. Let me be clear about what I'm saying. I do believe a man should be proud of who he is and what he stands for. However, I don't think it's necessary to flaunt your sexuality in an environment where others who have to be there may deem it disruptive, inappropriate or offensive... heyyy!!! Madea must die! I am not attacking the person. I am concerned about the image the character portrays.

There's a lot of uncertainty about what causes homosexuality. Some psychologists and researchers say it's psychological trauma, developmental difficulties during early childhood or early problems between father and son. Others suggest it's of genetic origin, noting discrepancies within the brain structure. Scientists disagree on the significance of biological and/or cultural influence on sexual orientation, gender, sexual behavior and transsexuality. *Newsweek* reporter David Gelman notes in his article, *Homosexuality: Born or Bred?* (February 24, 1992),

> In the gay community itself, many welcome the indication that gayness begins in the chromosomes. Theoretically, it could gain them civil-rights protection accorded any 'natural' minority.

Others however, are concerned that the identification of a genetic basis for homosexuality might fuel discrimination and "prompt efforts to tinker with the genetic code of gay adults or to test during pregnancy and abort potentially gay fetuses," wrote *Time* magazine reporter William A. Henry, III in *Born Gay?* (July 26, 1993).

Let me be crystal clear, I'm not homophobic or a gay basher. This dynamic affects my family just like it probably does yours. I can't talk about sexual behavior like it's just an act or action. We are talking about people, how to better understand our bodies and whether there's a method to our personal sexual desires.

Men have a higher number of sexually sensitive nerve endings in their bodies because they spend an exorbitant amount of time pursuing mates.

Testosterone (the male hormone) is associated with competition and masculinity while estrogen (the female hormone) is associated with social skills and nurturing.

Although kissing can appear innocent, it is in many ways the foundation of intimacy. The lips and the mouth are erotically charged body parts. They can be used to explore, stimulate and excite the body. The first tongue-kiss is regarded as a touchstone, a rite of passage, the beginning of manhood for some young men, the entry to adult sexuality; while for the elderly, pleasuring, touching or fondling becomes the mantra of eroticism. The seniors still want to talk a good game. I hear them out in public calling each other out, talking over the youngsters heads... talkin-bout, *Honey if you give me a little fellatio, I'll give you some cunnilingus, then we will negotiate the coitus.* And every now and again, she will zing him right back with, *I see you've been taking your medicine!* I know what they're talking about. They're not fooling me.

Speaking of fooling somebody, let me send a word of caution out to ladies who like to pleasure yourself by way of petting (outer-course) or should I say massaging your erogenous zones for sexual stimulation and orgasm. Especially the ladies who are *hooked-on-tronics*, those who secretly own every kind of electronic and battery-operated toy they can hide: massagers, vibrators, a couple of dildos that don't really do anything; they are forced to do some things they aren't so proud of. And to make it even more challenging for a man she wears an eight-hour insertion remotely controlled, set on a timer. So when you hear her yell out at work behind her cubicle, it's not going to be because she made the sale, closed a deal or anything like that, oh no, her timer probably just kicked in. Some of you shake the hell out of your clitoris, you know that? Stop using those high-powered massagers. That's too much vibration for your poor little vulva! The poor thing is growing muscles around it trying to protect itself from you! It won't even shut down or close up anymore and the clit just stares out at us in disgust, trembling and shaking her little head like it has Parkinson's. Then an innocent man comes along, ambitious and spry, trying to be all he can be, not knowing he's got a *helluva-act* to follow. But if you want your man to be the one who lights your fire, you're going to have to put some of those things down for real-doh... and no, I didn't say dildo.

But seriously, men are taking all kinds of medications and drugs, snorting, smoking, drinking and going blind trying to find ways to avoid disappointing you. So let's be fair, take your clitoris off steroids and electronica, give us a chance. Go back to the way it used to be when you would blow up like a martyr and he lived as a single witness. That's why fantasizing about sex is the most popular of all sexual and erotic behaviors. It is the one time a man can explore uninhibited passion and lust in his mind. Over is the mentality of living in the good old days, when sex was innocent even if you didn't know the person; when the worst thing that could happen was you left a baby seed behind that you didn't have to take care of because the village helped raise the children. In these times, with HIV and AIDS standing as a much more serious consequence than even unwanted pregnancy, we can still joke about sex... but we need to also not lose sight of the fact that it can *literally kill you.*

Yes this is a new day. Men are held responsible for their sexual behavior by law enforcement agencies, and by their women and children. The law and standards on sexual behavior are very serious in themselves. So I'm sure many guys have learned to behave themselves sexually and you would give them a passing grade. Let's see, the average guy would probably get a letter grade of "B" and not much lower than a "C" for his sexual behavior, 'cause the boys know they can't make too many mistakes. But if he's *driving a hard bargain* he may get some "As" from ladies. Or is that just my particular fantasy? Some men say sex is one of the most powerful forces on earth... the magic seems to happen for just a few seconds, for *all that it's worth.*

12

Enjoying Love without Marriage

Learn how times are changing

There is no other relationship like a marital relationship – a social and legal contract that attempts to guarantee two people will commit to each other for life. There is a certain amount of dare associated with this union. Marriage is by nature a multifaceted institution. We can define it as a legal commitment between two people to share emotional and physical intimacy, various work or professional undertakings and economic resources. Although people typically think of marriage as a union of a man and a woman, many same-sex couples are interested in marrying. This definition of marriage can be applied to same-sex couples, except that there are no legal commitments in all but a handful states. In earlier generations, adults had fewer choices and society assumed that everyone who didn't marry faced loneliness and disapproval. Today, the number of never-married adults has increased dramatically, reflecting a change in social consciousness, preferences and attitudes.

A survey sponsored by the *American Community Survey* shows that more than 30 million Americans live by themselves, which accounts for more than a quarter of all households and nearly 13 percent of the nation's total population. For the first time ever, one-person households outnumber married couples with children, with more women being single than men. According to the *American Association for Single People*, an unmarried majority has emerged in many American cities. Only 42.2 percent of blacks age 18 years or older were married, while more than one-third (38 percent) have never been married; among Hispanics, slightly more than 30 percent have never married, and among whites, the figure is 22.1 percent. From 1970 to 2003, the proportion of 25 to 29-year-old Americans who reported themselves as never married quadrupled, from 11 percent to 47.5 percent. During that same period, 22 percent of whites were listed as never-married; while for blacks and Hispanics during that three-decade-long window, it was 39 percent and 30 percent, respectively. We also know that with actions such as leaving the marriage forever and vowing never to get married again, your distaste for your mate can be so strong that you never want to contact him again, even for the divorce. For that reason and others, the divorce statistic is closer to 60 percent for all nationalities. Much research supports the idea that never-married women are better off than their male counterparts.

So who are these single people? From my experience we have the following categories of singles:

    1. Voluntary: never married and not looking,

2. Involuntary: never married, actively seeking, widowed,

3. Fear of marriage: negative observations, perceptions and experiences such as being raised in an unhappy household where the parents frequently fought,

4. Prefer to marry: never had the guts, finances or chance with the right person.

In my opinion the advantages of being single may be:

1. Greater opportunity for self-development, personal growth and fulfillment,

2. Opportunities to meet different people, to develop or enjoy different friendships,

3. Personal and financial independence, self-sufficiency and responsibility, more variety of sexual pleasures and erotic experiences,

4. Freedom to control your life,

5. More opportunity for career change, development and expansion.

The advantages of being single relate to having increased freedom; freedom from having to take care of a man or family (children); freedom to do as you please how and when you want; freedom of not having to answer to others in terms of time, behaviors, decisions, interests and commitment. Some women don't want to invest so much of their time and energy trying to cultivate a relationship with no real assurance that he'll be there in the future. Even with all of your preparation and experience, there is no guarantee.

Conversely, the disadvantages of being single are generally:

1. Possible loneliness and lack of companionship,
2. Experiencing economic hardship,
3. Feeling out of place in social gatherings,
4. Sexual insecurity, lack of children or a family in which to bring them up,
5. No tax breaks,
6. The lack of trust in relations.

The absence of a partner or prospective partner is associated with loneliness; however, loneliness occurs within marriage as well. Research (Torstam, 1992, in DeGenova) has found that 40 percent of married people reported being lonely often or sometimes, 16 percent said they felt lonely even when they were with others and 7 percent said they were lonely all the time. Women were more likely to indicate feeling lonely than were men, particularly married women 20 to 49 years of age. Women may simply have higher expectations for companionship within marriage that are not being met. Many single women have unresolved or unrecognized ambivalence about their status, and simultaneously experience feelings of loss and grief. Most women I interviewed want to be married, though some didn't. Some blame themselves, but most blame men. Single women who blame themselves fall primarily into the fear category:

1. Physical: felt unattractive, overweight, special needs,
2. Personality: shyness, lack of social skills, dependence or independence, nonsubmissive or subservient, domineering,
3. Psychological: low self-esteem, abused as a child, codependency, lack of confidence,
4. Career: want to focus on themselves, job advancement, personal goals.

Single women who blamed men complained that those they were meeting couldn't handle their intelligence, accomplishments, confidence, assertiveness or financial status. The most frequently cited drawbacks to not being married were the absence of being special to a man, having to be the rock, lack of feelings for a man, the absence of family and children, the sadness of growing old alone and the absence of someone to take care of you as you grow old or become ill.

Unhealthy and unhappy people are less likely to get married. On the other hand, people who have superior health and physical well-being have a greater possibility of being married. However, the stress of divorce, separation or death of a spouse may draw against one's health. So if the question is *do married people live a happier and healthier life?*, the answer is not necessarily. Marital

- 150 -   BARRY FLETCHER

status is just one of many variables affecting a person's well-being.

I never understood why women are so anxious about signing their life over to a partnership that has only about a 24 percent chance of being successful. Close to 60 percent of these partnerships end in divorce, 75 percent of the couples that stay in the marriage for more than 10 years are bored stiff or unhappy and fewer than 20 percent of this previous group would say they are happy. Most women don't feel complete unless they try it once because they equate that with children and raising a family. In my experience from talking with men, I believe they make their decisions about marriage under the influence of lust, sex and the anticipation of more of both. Well of course this would require a responsible man, and this is where many of you ladies begin adding your checklists to the mix: background check, financial and credit check, full physical check, relationship with God check and any past relationship check! But if you're really desperate to get married, you know you can run off to Vegas and make it happen very quickly. Being "pressed to get married" is something I see as a female thing.

You show me a man who is pressed to get married and I'll show you a man who needs to be taken care of. He's the baby's daddy, or going to the Army, or he can't afford the house, the car and the clothes, or he's afraid to be alone or just can't stand to see you with someone else. None of these are good reasons to get married. There lies the irony inherent in the idea of the "marriage union." A man who is fast to jump into this type of union could easily be the man who wants to control you from the time you sign the "con"-tract. What's more disturbing is the preacher who would marry you – two or three times. You go to him the first time, swear to God that you'll love and protect your intended for the rest of your life, no matter what happens to the two of you... only later to find yourself going to your lawyer, swearing that you can't live with him anymore. But then, once again, you find another man and off you go to the preacher and swear to God *again* that you'll stay with *this* man for the rest of your life. Well who's the bigger sinner, you or the preacher? Marriage is the most demanding relationship there is, and rarely does the couple plan for failure. For that reason, I don't think that anyone should be able to get married until about age 30, and even then they should only be allowed to get married once, if you really want to make the union concrete.

This is one of the reasons I never committed to the union, because I actually take any vows and commitment made to and before God seriously. One of my desperate-to-get-married clients suggested to me that you can change the vows to not say, "UNTIL DEATH DO YOU PART." My reply was, "well then, you might as well take out the part about FOR RICHER OR FOR POORER for that matter, 'cause if the eagles are flying over my head and not into my bank account, the marriage is already dead... those eagles could turn into vultures!"

Many people of faith have multiple marriages, which is kind of suggestive to me. How many times do you swear to God? Take away the 15 minutes of wedding ceremony with fame, glory, lights, camera and action, and you would likely have fewer people marrying. One thing is for sure: people don't seem to have money for funerals but they sure do manage to find it for weddings. Nostalgia: the good old days, when thoughts and memories seem right because they were familiar. Old thoughts of marriage appeal to us because they simplify complex issues into plain black and white imagery. We embrace the old teachings or philosophies because they reflect a better, kinder world. However, clinging to the powerful past because these were the times when "marriages lasted" is kind of sad. Focusing in on "the good old days" often comes at the expense of your living in the NOW; you run the risk of reflecting on what amounts to fantasies of how we wish things could be, not how they really are. We hold these truths to be self-evident. They are extremely powerful and pervasive because they have been drilled into us from a very early age by our parents, grandparents, teachers, preachers and society-at-large – even if you know in your heart that you want more from a marriage than what your parents or grandparents had.

Without a doubt, women have experienced accelerated change over the past 40 years in terms of equality, opportunity, status and freedom. Women have become more independent, more financially secure, less home-struck, less likely to tolerate discomfort and more inclined to leave a bad relationship. A good relationship encourages fairness, sharing, thoughtfulness, caring, and lots of respect. When you think about your parents' marriage or relationship, which or how many of these values did or does their relationship reflect?

As a child, I learned how to act by observing what actually happened in the household. That's right: actions speak louder than words. I was so dependent on my parents for love, encouragement and acceptance that I learned from them what to expect from love. I learned the difference between what they *said* and what they *did*; their differences in tolerance and behavior; what was respectful and disrespectful; what was wanted, needed, desired and accepted; and what was normal vs. what was outrageous. I learned my family culture without anybody directly teaching me. I learned it by watching how they acted. I watched Pop act out in impulsive anger, while Mom's rebellion and passive submission took many forms; I heard all the verbal threats between the two. The entire time I was crying out loud, whining, pouting and screaming at the top of my lungs for my parents' love and affection. Oftentimes, my mother would shy away from conflict in the interest of preserving the marriage. However, couples in a healthy relationship should face issues straight on, rather than avoid the challenges of love and commitment. It's the ability to communicate that keeps a marriage strong.

As an adult, I am still learning by observation through my work as a hair designer. I've learned that people in general have five basic needs in their lives: professional, physical, intellectual, emotional and spiritual. The more of these needs we have satisfied, the more balance we bring into our lives. More often people are happy to get at least three of them satisfied.

Out of desperation, couples sometime wish they could go back to the good old days when things were much less complex... a kinder, simpler world; days when people hung onto clichés and old sayings to get them through hard times and bitter emotions. Which of the following have you held onto?

1. If loving you is wrong, I don't want to be right,
2. Love will conquer all,
3. If it feels good, it must be good,
4. The love you give is the pleasure you get,
5. You have to make some sacrifices for the one you love,
6. Love is from the heart and doesn't take much work,
7. You shouldn't say things that may hurt feelings,
8. Hold back on the glazed donuts and he'll change,
9. Most people know the difference between right and wrong,
10. Two people in love will agree on most things,
11. It's a thin line between love and hate,
12. It's best not to express your anger,
13. It takes a fool to learn that love don't love nobody,
14. Let's stay together for the good times,

15. You'll never find someone who'll love
you like I do.

These are some of the terms that unhealthy relationships are built on. Not to say that these ideas are wrong all the time and that it's not noble to sacrifice for love. I just want to caution you about integrating these ideas into your train of thought as common sense, psychological acceptance, emotional awareness or some type of logistic equation to help you make concrete decisions. Maybe some of this worked back in the day. After all, it was folks back in the day that thought of these sayings!

My personal favorite was included in an R&B song from the 1970s, "Who's making love to your old lady while you were out making love?" My father hated that song, and for that reason we couldn't play it in our house. Nostalgia, that's what it is, the good old days when people got married and made it work, the days when marriage had more meaning to the couple. Couples today have a lot more challenges. Women are more outspoken, emotional and forthright these days – sometimes to the level where men are afraid to say what they are really thinking to try to preserve the peace. Men are walking around with stuff on their minds they only wished their lady knew... but they fear bringing it up.

It's a new day with many new ways to cultivate a relationship. We must first throw out the old blueprints and start like a chef does when preparing a good, healthy meal... he or she works from scratch. The younger you are, the more choices you have and the more profoundly your decisions affect your future. The challenge for the new generation is accelerated change, overwhelming complexity and tremendous competition. The way we relate is evolving, relations are open to expression, fairness and equality amongst equals. With this comes new beliefs and teachings, based on wisdom and myths from an earlier age. What matters now is teaching that reflects the issues we face today, and shared needs and ideas that are healthier, nurturing and beneficial to learning each other.

It's okay to allow yourself to be vulnerable, admit your mistakes and openly recognize your weaknesses. It's good for couples to express a full range of emotions, shortcomings and even anger. It's the new high self-esteem. Feeling and expressing love, and consideration and respect for your mate seem to rule the day. Show sincere willingness to address issues and negotiate amicable solutions. Make long-term goals together, bond through shared experiences, have lots of fun together and reminisce about past fun you've had together. Don't be afraid to try new things sexually or otherwise together. Find the right time for soul-searching and speaking from the heart while continuing to remind each other of your affection and what love has to do with it.

According to Dr. William Glasser, M.D., marriage has five basic needs. In his book, *Getting Together and Staying Together*, he writes:

"With the possible exception of angering, we have no built-in behaviors. We have to learn everything we do, and the motivation for this learning is our pleasure and painful feelings. The better we do it, the better we feel, and this doing better and feeling better is the driving force behind all human progress. A huge amount of human activity is devoted to thinking about sex and doing it. But we believe that if more married people understood that they are driven by the five basic needs and, by using choice theory, making an effort in their marriage from the start to satisfy themselves, we could begin to make some significant progress in improving marriage.

Survival:

In modern America, most people are assured of survival if they make any effort at all. Few people die of starvation or because they don't have a home. In many marriages the most common symptom of differences in the need to survive is fighting about money. This may be a good time to exercise choice theory; basically, choice theory explains that the only person we can control is ourselves. The partner almost always changes as we rid ourselves of external control. We should do all we can to make it as easy as possible to satisfy his or her needs. To do this we should start submitting to the seven caring habits of choice theory: (1) listening, (2) supporting, (3) encouraging, (4) respecting, (5) trusting, (6) accepting, and (7) always negotiating disagreements. The power of choice theory is that it helps you get along with other people, especially people close to you.

Love and belonging:

Women, probably based on their role as mothers, seem to be endowed with a stronger need to love and belong than men. In the beginning of marriage, many partners, especially women, are fooled by sex into believing that the men love them more than they actually do. This is because for women, unlike men, sex is more genetically tied to their need for love than their need to survive. A man with a strong survival need wants a lot of sex and, in the beginning, acts lovingly to get it. There are many individual variations of the need for love and belonging that tend to make marriage a mystery. Many women and men are very loving towards children yet seem unable to love an adult with the same intensity.

Fun:

The need that is most easily satisfied in marriage, fun is a need that we can satisfy by ourselves or with others. It can be satisfied in many ways, at so many places, and at almost any time of day or night. Fun doesn't require sex, money, great effort, or good health; all it requires is that they start doing again what they did so much of together before they got married. Fun has great staying power. Sex and even love may wane over a long marriage, but fun remains fresh because unlike sex, it can always go off in a new direction. There are almost no restrictions on having fun. Sometimes later in life interests can transform the relationship.

Freedom:

As a rule, people with a low need for freedom are much happier in marriage. Negotiating freedom is perhaps the most difficult of all marital negotiations; women can teach men to be more loving and caring but you can't teach a man to give up his freedom. To ask people to give up more freedom than they are capable of giving is to ask them to suffer more pain than the marriage may be worth to them. The only hope in this scenario is if the need for love and belonging overrides the need for freedom.

Power:

Animals may fight for a territory, to protect their young, or for a mate to pass on their genes, but they do not fight, as we do, just for the sake of power. And for having our way, or punishing another for disagreeing with us, there is no human relationship more contentious than marriage. Why this is so and how it can

be avoided is the key to solving the
mystery of marriage. For any partnership
to succeed – and marriage is no exception
– the partners need to be friends to be
able to enjoy each other's company.
Much more than sex and love, friendship
is based on equal power or no power, and
equal power is based on listening to each
other and really paying attention. There is
no other way!"

So those are Dr. Glasser's five needs of a marriage
– and I can't get past the first need on the list! I feel the
need for *love* more than I do for *marriage*. Am I wrong
for that? In my relationships with women, I'm not at all
competitive about power. Sometimes you like a little
intestinal fortitude, it keeps you fresh and keeps your
wits about you. In my business, women have every
opportunity to exercise their power or to relinquish it to
the 'authority.' As a cosmetological image-maker and
hairdresser, I have an opportunity to make some very
important decisions about a person's outer presence...
talking about external control. However that person still
retains veto power. Power or control is given when trust
is present. I've been working on, for, and with women
most of my life, and I still can't tell you how they are,
because that might change by tomorrow. One thing is
for sure, ladies you have every right to make your own
choices and decide what really makes you happy in life.
Hey, get what you want out of life, married or single. I
can't tell you how many people I've met who are

secretly unhappy with their marriage or significant other. I'm not trying to bring up thought-provoking ambivalence about marriage out of being a hater. I just wonder sometimes, "What in the hell were some of you thinking when you decided to get married?"

Here's a little secret I want to share with you. Most men want to be in a committed relationship, but I mean committed in that the *woman* is committed and loyal to *him*. But when it's time to secure that commitment with a signature, some men transform those ringing wedding bells into... let freedom ring. Let freedom ring for as long as I can hear the chimes, until I can't stall her anymore. His next move is to buy you a rock, and he already knows that doing so will get him up to two years of engagement. That's when the countdown begins! See, you ladies are wrong for this. After you get the ring on your finger, you start changing, knowing he just spent all the money he had on you. Now you're acting all chipper, making kind gestures and being all caring and everything. You start saying stuff like: "You can drive my car baby. I'm going to get you a house key made honey. Let me know when you want something to eat." News flash: Brothers know how to *sice'm on up and stroke em on down*, while you wait anxiously for something that may never happen... 'cause you want it so bad. Careful what you ask for – you just might get it! Hey, I'm just happy to be a man. Don't get me wrong, I love you ladies. It's just that some of you are never satisfied unless a man is making your heart beat faster, and you really don't have such a great choice for pickings. This is the reason so many men want to savor their freedom while women, on the other hand, having found (what you think is) a good man, want him secured, committed... whipped. Let me tell you some other news, ladies... you can't handle the truth!

A passionate, committed relationship can be even more enjoyable than marriage. It's voluntary. That's what keeps it hot, which gives freedom to expression of how you really feel about your boo. What I'm trying to tell you is, maybe it's time to try a little tenderness. Listen, Steve Harvey has already told you it's all right to act like a lady, but you still gotta think like a freaking man! Or think for him! That's my dog!

Oprah Winfrey had a segment on her show dedicated to the 70 percent of black women who are single. Oprah is not married, says she never wanted to get married and also thinks that ladies shouldn't hold out for marriage. Live your best life, she says. You folks with these dysfunctional marriages are taking up too much time in church, worrying the preachers too much about your personal stuff. The ministers are there to help save lives and possibly save someone's soul, and you want them to save your marriage. Ministers are not marriage counselors – that is a social issue.

I was reading the August 2009 issue of Essence magazine and ran across this article "Single and Satisfied" by Bishop T.D. Jakes. In this essay, Jakes wants you to find the joys and possibilities in flying solo. He says fun-loving people "start the party before any guest arrives." He even suggested you should start dating yourself. In other words, back off a bit, just leave him alone, he's had it with all of these social problems and only wants you to fall in love with God. He's already done a background check on Him, but can't tell you much about the guy you married. And wouldn't you know? The very day after I read that article by Bishop Jakes, I received a nice e-mail presentation written by T.D. Jakes, and I thought, what a coincidence! Until I opened the e-mail and saw that the article was titled "Let's Just Kiss and Say Good-Bye." My thought was that he's really trying to get a message out to people struggling with their social life and marriage.

Let's take a little time to examine why marriage isn't working for some couples. Well, we haven't made polygamy legal in this country. However, it is legal in many parts of Africa, the Middle East and Asia, with some living all one house and some in other situations where each wife has a separate household. I'm sure there would be many men in this country who would approve of a polygamous family, based on some of the stories I've heard! Open marriage is another idea couples are trying. This is sometimes known as "swinging together" and is beginning to take on an interesting twist. At the root of most failing marriages is poor communication, which causes the anger, tension and intolerable frustration. Effective communication involves the ability to exchange ideas, feelings, beliefs, facts and attitudes so that the message from the sender is accurately heard and interpreted by the receiver, and vice versa.

A marriage lives and breathes on admiration, respect, companionship, affection, honesty, trust, fidelity, responsibility and the ability to handle crises and pressure, just to name a few important characteristics. Some of us would have to go to a career training school to learn all of that stuff. Most couples are influenced by the characteristics of their family of origin. What you see is what you get. Some people choose the wrong partner as a result of socio-cultural factors that might influence their marital qualities; especially age, status, income, education, job title, ethnicity, class and reputation. Others pick the wrong partner because they read too many fairy tales and watch too many movies, so much so that they are just in a fantasy world. Some women fall into the trap of disregarding the true personal qualities of a man. They focus instead on the physical qualities, get caught up in how good he looks and do not peep his ability to be responsible or stable. Some ladies boost their ego by choosing a significant other who will entertain them and enhance their image.

Nevertheless and most importantly, the partners have to be happy if the marriage is to be considered successful. If you want to break it down in phases, there's a premarital phase, a first-year phase, and an after-the-first-child-is-born phase. Research shows that money is often the culprit of problems at all three phases, but lack of intercourse, poor temperament, jealousy and lack of space came in close behind as being the causes of marriages failing.

You know what? Marriage is too damn complicated. Two people who have two different purposes, directions, and ideas have to somehow mold into one. People say you have to *work* on marriage. I'm trying not to work that hard to be happy. It's just not that serious. I get along with everyone, have plenty of fun and love my freedom. Hate me if you want to, but some of the most powerful women who are making a difference in our lives today are single: Oprah, Condoleezza Rice, Sonia Sotomayor, Halle Berry, Martha Stewart, Barbara Walters, Kathy Hughes and Dr. Maya Angelou, to name a few. I just don't understand why so many women are so bent out of shape to get married. Women are willing to relocate, change jobs and make major sacrifices just to get a man! Even Chastity Bono changed her sex... so that she, too, can get married.

13

The Good Men: Where Are They?

What kind of women do they respect?

What do you really want, ladies? Is a good man that hard to find, or is it just that *you* have a hard time finding him? First, you say good men are hard to find, then you say all men are dogs and then you cry, *Who let the dogs out?"* Please ladies, don't get it twisted. Do not confuse a good man with a wealthy or good-looking man. Looks are only a start. They act as a vehicle of awareness, a pathway to attraction or to a tantalizing, alluring impression. The power of magnetism causes many women to settle for men who look good, the kind who makes for some scrumptious arm candy when she is out on the town; a good-looking man who prompts your friends, family and coworkers to wonder, "How did she meet him? What does he do for a living?" He seems like the kind of man whose stellar looks convince you that he is an intelligent, well-mannered gentleman with lots of potential, until he opens his mouth and removes all doubt. Then it becomes time for you to decide: Is arm-candy all that I want? Is this good-looking man, who ain't got two cents to rub together, really the best fit for me? Fact is, most of us are inclined to judge a book by its cover, initially.

A man has a keen sense for judging your vulnerabilities. By watching your body language, he can tell when he has you reeling. At that point, he knows he can have his way. Other times, with the independent woman, her disposition may read *defense,* as if she must protect her emotions from the potential hurt of deceit. She's more determined to meet a man who would share her vision and values. She may have the mindset of "been there, done that, can take it or leave it," then she is the type who will take some convincing.

Then there is the independent type, a woman who is really not looking to live with a man. Let's just say she's not pressed, can do bad all by herself and enjoys her personal time of solitude. And let's not leave out the needy woman, Miss High Maintenance. Her attitude is, "You have to give to receive... and give and give and give some more... Nothing from nothing leaves nothing." Ladies, whichever of these represents your particular outlook, it is always best to find peace and refuge within yourself before letting a man into your life.

Relationships are built on enduring qualities, not superficial external factors like looks, money or material things that could change in a blink and affect your compatibility. The true foundation for intimacy is a combination of trust, compassion, affection, and mutual respect. Women who have a sense of direction and a clear strategy for obtaining their goals will exude confidence, which is sexy in and of itself.

Don't be afraid to ask defining questions at the beginning such as: "I'm curious, what kind of woman do you respect?"

    a. "What are your goals for establishing a relationship with me?"

    b. "What are some of the things you feel you need to improve about yourself?"

You should develop questions that would help you understand his values, his goals in life and his plans for accomplishing them. Although these may be general characteristics, it is important to know a man's ideals, educational background, professional interests, spiritual beliefs, hobbies and special interests. Hearing his philosophy on life will definitely help you identify some of the things you may have in common. It is also always smart to understand and appreciate your companion's views because you're not going to change him much where his fundamental beliefs are concerned. A woman can influence a man to a certain degree but she can't teach him patience, thoughtfulness, genuine courtesy and respect for others, especially when it comes to his interactions with parents, the elderly and children.

One of the biggest complaints I have heard women express about men is that they are selfish and don't listen with consideration and concern. Learning effective communication skills, and how and when to compromise, is an ongoing process. In some instances, it will help you identify the "work-ability" of the relationship. Remember, your search for a good man and intimacy begins with *you* – and with an honest assessment of your own social and personal development and needs. Partnership has always been about teamwork, not just exclusively about him or you. Again, to thine own self be true. But at the same time, we all have to give up some aspects of *self* for the good of a *union*. It doesn't matter if you're dating or are in a committed relationship, sacrifice is required.

The selection process for dating is always an emotional risk. It doesn't matter how long you've been dating or how experienced you are, there will always be a multitude of complex issues, concerns and emotions involved with pairing and partnering. No one wants to get their feelings hurt on a date while negotiating attractions, discussing interests and comparing values, but they might as well be prepared for it. Getting hurt is just a natural part of the vetting process.

I will also tell you some other peculiarities about dating that you might want to watch out for: the elements of uncertainty, excitement and optimism. You should find excitement in these basic unanswered questions, at least initially: *Could he possibly be Mr. Right, my life partner? Will he turn Me into We?* But before you get to that point, here is a larger and more important question that you should consider: *What is a good man anyway?* I think definitions vary; it depends on whom you ask. Ask a man's grandmother, and she might say that he is a responsible fella who works hard and takes care of his family. His mother may refer to him as a gentleman, a guy who finished college, embarked upon a career, the kind of son she hopes will find a nice wife and "bring her home some grand kids."

His sister might say of her brother, "That's my buddy there; he looks out for me, advises me and protects me." His girlfriend may suggest that he's a funny guy to be around, to hang out with, a man who is good in bed. The wife may easily answer, "He's my first, my last, my everything and my good man means the world to me. He's loving, thoughtful, generous, caring, smart, ambitious, trustworthy, reliable, sexy and makes me feel whole." His mistress may say he's attractive, gives good love and is very private. And they could all be right, which is what makes this phase of your deliberations so complicated. Good and bad men usually share many of the same qualities and tendencies. It is very rare that a single man (or woman for that matter) is truly "all bad" or "all good." For this reason, I suggest you spend time getting to know the man's heart. It is the nucleus of his soul and is connected to his emotions, deepest feelings and thoughts.

For those of you who want to know where to find a good man, I would say, right under your nose. We are everywhere – except, well, maybe you won't find us in the ladies room! But seriously, stop looking for a man. Start looking happy and satisfied with yourself and he will tap you on your shoulder. Do not despair about where the "good men" hang out, because the options are endless.

Folks are signing up by the millions for online social networks in large part because they are finding lots of success with dating web sites. Some of these sites can help you avoid wasting time on people with whom you have nothing in common. Others still prefer the tried-and-true venues for meeting people: the gym, social outings, through friends' referrals, church, grocery stores, clubs, parties, work, etc. Sometimes it only takes a smile to send clues to the man that you are interested. My advice on this front? Be ready to meet a man every time you leave your house. Look and feel your best each and every time you hit the front door and start out on that errand, to church or for your day at work. And be careful about trying to meet someone who is too much like you, especially if you feel you are lacking excitement and adventure. I mean, if you want someone who is just like you, why don't you date yourself? There have to be different dimensions and dynamics, harmony and discord, righteousness and submission in a relation to keep it hot!

Human nature provides a multitude of competing wills. On the one hand, we want to be acknowledged for our unique accomplishments and identity. On the other hand, we are working to unite with a life partner. Human nature, as with all living entities, includes a basic drive to perpetuate life. Very often a man is cued in by a woman's physical appearance and attributes, like a code of conduct.

Let me tell you something that is deeper than meeting your ultimate mate in the most peculiar way. It's the amount of information you can exchange in a short period of time. Quite a bit can be discovered over a cup of coffee, enough to form a conscious opinion about a person. The two of you naturally have your antennas up while indulging in a conversation; all the while, your respective sensitivity radar equipment is scanning the energy level, checking for assertiveness, kindness, mannerisms, hygiene, and mental acuity. I guess it's fair to say that from a cerebral perspective, the brain accumulates information, feelings and emotions, shuttles it through and processes it, then advises us how to relate, so that we can make good, clear conscious decisions about our partners or potential mates.

If you decide what you want to know about a person, a huge amount of information can be obtained from just a short conversation – if you talk about the right things. The one trait a man's radar will like the most in you is KINDNESS. A man can read a lot into kindness – it spells 'keeper.' A kind woman is wife material. It is one of the unspoken attributes that, for most men, is very compelling and thought-provoking. When a man is looking for a future wife, he'll look past the physical features to less tangible assets: character, kindness, personality, attitude, honesty and intellect. His standards change dramatically when he's looking for someone with whom to build a life and make a living. He'll find you, and it'll be in the right place at the right time, as if it was meant to be, or like it was heaven-sent. Sometimes, it is the way you look him in his eyes that makes him see merriment.

Self-confidence communicates strength and is very sexy to a righteous man who has integrity, and is not afraid of commitment. He sees your self-confidence as favorably translating to domesticity, also toward your ability to contribute to the family income, both of which are necessary to ensure thriving relationships in these times. People should spend more time trying to *be* the right mate, as opposed to *looking for* the right mate. You have to define your own life and be secure within yourself. Often times our self-esteem is tied to whether we have a sex partner or not, which may cause us to settle for less than we deserve.

Additionally, we must guard against making the common mistake of acting out of fear. It is part of human nature that one of the most powerful motivators within us is fear; fear of not being attractive or strong, fear of being hurt or alone, fear of weakness and rejection. But in reality, what is fear exactly? **F**alsified **E**vidence **A**ppearing **R**eal, which by another name is just paranoia. Fear will strip you of your strength and power (which are subjective) and the balance of the two can shift with every situation.

At the end of the day, one of the biggest stumbling blocks to a successful relationship is something we all think about, but usually have problems discussing: money and finances. However, the success of a romantic relation rests on friendship. When you ask where all the good men are, perhaps you are, in reality, avoiding a more important question: Why would a happily single guy who could have sex with you, move in with you, and have his way with you decide to legally bind himself to you in marriage? If you have not become pregnant by him, why would he give up his freedom, share his wealth and commit himself to the uncertainties of cohabiting with you if he doesn't have to? What do you bring to the relationship that he cannot receive somewhere else? What is unique and special about you that distinguishes you in a positive way?

I'm not saying this is always the case, I'm just asking you to look at his reasons for appearing to be resistant to the idea of "settling down" (if this is the situation you encounter). While his reasons might seem good or bad, from your perspective it is probably more important to think deeply about your own role, and about what you can control regarding of your own behavior and responses. Before you start to believe you are irresistible and that your relationship is framed by unconditional love, take an honest look at your good man – and at the signals and signs you may be sending.

Friendship is a magnificent thing. It can turn commitment-phobia into a loving foundation if you both are sincere and want the same things out of life. The real soul searching starts within. As easy as that is to say, it can be difficult to achieve. But the burden of truth lies with you, because you are the only one you can control.

A man may be considered good if he fulfills most of your needs, but at the same time, you must realize that no one woman can meet 100 percent of a man's needs. This is primarily because most men have diverse needs that just can't all be addressed by one woman, even if she is "the best." It is incumbent upon you to ask him what his needs are, and then give him as many of those needs as you can, and to also help him feel secure by giving him the space and the pressure-free environment to allow him to have all (or most) of his remaining needs met – within reason, of course. For example, if your man is into golf, why hassle him if he wants to spend part of each weekend out on the links? It is about finding balance, within reason. ('Cause I am not trying to tell you that it is okay if your man says his "needs" include *getting some* now and again from the neighbor lady down the street. If you are not open with that then change or let him know, and be prepared to send him packing!)

On the positive side, you may secure him by helping him feel complete, important, protected, supported and most of all, happy. Don't judge a good man by what he can do for you but by how he makes you feel about yourself. It is a positive circle effect, in which your ability to feel secure about yourself allows you to let your man feel secure about himself – and about the two of you, together. Remember: You have the power. And in his mind he needs you more than you need him, even if admitting it can sometimes be difficult for him. You are a prize and you are worthy of his pursuit. Never present yourself as easy to get... a good man would know that.

14

If Jesus Were One of Us?

There's a Jesus-like man for every woman

This chapter is in no way an attempt to preach the gospel or challenge anyone's religious or spiritual beliefs. I didn't think a book titled *Learn a Man, Earn a Man* should overlook one who most would claim to be the greatest of all time. So if the man I describe in this chapter doesn't sound like your Jesus, your Jehovah, your God, then remember that my goal is in no way to offend but simply to explore possibilities, stretch the imagination and perhaps even educate.

From the intelligent to the idiot, the rich to the poor, the invalid to the healthy, at some point in our lives we all will understandably have a problem with faith in God. It is our fault. men fail. We collectively fail to live a religious life that is not contradictory, blasphemous or hypocritical. We fail in our separatist doctrines that promote our personal preferences instead of giving glory to God. There is no middle ground and folks are more afraid of being wrong than being happy. God created us all in His image, so it is only our failings that keep us stuck on division. When a follower of Christ acts and works like Jesus, he has the image of the

Son in his mind and in his heart. But it can be so hard to help others learn and understand. Sometimes, folks cannot move past all that they have seen, heard and survived.

Jesus was the strongest, coolest brother who ever lived. He was always at a party, always eating with friends and regular people. He shunned protocol and did his best to be humble at every turn. He was the Son of the Creator of the Universe. He had his head on straight; you couldn't trick Him, get Him off His mission or stop Him. He was born in a stable. This is not a big deal if you realize that God created the whole world. It's like us sitting in our underwear in the living room. It is your house. He got dinged for talking to "sinners": tax collectors, poor people, floozies and the downtrodden. He didn't hang with the big shots because they either didn't need or want Him.

Jesus is spirit incarnate, the strength of power, the ruler of all kingdoms (the here and present and the past and then the future). Jesus exemplifies the belief that virtue and divine inspiration can never be separated. Man on the other hand is created in the image and the likeness of God – and made of flesh, which is where our weaknesses reside.

The spiritual man is a visionary who believes his life is a gift he should revere. He is willing and able to reform himself into the ultimate perfection of excellence that would reign him supreme over all humanly matters. Most importantly, he cherishes his relationship with God. He believes Jesus is his personal savior and is devoted to leaving the world a better place as a result of his having been a part of it. God knew from the beginning that in order to mold us into the image of Himself, He would have to shape our life experiences along the lines of Jesus' experiences. We look at our lives and see His Son then look at His Son and see our lives.

Everyone has their own interpretation of Jesus and how He will appear when He returns. The Bible says Jesus is the exact likeness of God. We as humans will never be that exact same likeness because, unlike Jesus who was fully man and fully God, we are simply fully man. So don't try and act like you don't need Jesus, for He's the only one who could save you from you and you only have your lifetime to find him.

But remember, ordinary man has the potential to spiritually look like Jesus. In other words, the man in your life whom you call your "Boo" could very well be a Jesus-like man too. The question is, would you recognize him if you saw him? Would you pick up on his kind gestures? Can you detect a good heart? Can he be part of your life or could you even be his wife? Your Jesus-like man is the perfect man for you in every way. If Christ lives in him, he has Christ-likeness. It's not so important that he looks like Christ in today's time, as long as he's willing and able to continue the work that Jesus started, fulfilling the great mission of saving souls, helping people feel good about themselves and feel love in their time and space, on earth as it is in heaven. Selah.

I don't know how many "Jesus-like" men there are walking around in the world today, but I do know that they are probably outnumbered by the "Satan-like" who also walk among us.

There are countless people in the world today who are very caring and kind-hearted to others, i.e., Jesus-like. These people make a positive difference in others' lives by exercising their faith in humanity, being willing to lend a helping hand, and making volunteerism a worthy and popular endeavor. But who am I to judge how much of Jesus a man has in him, or how much man Jesus had in him for that matter? But I'm happy to tell you that I know men who have a heart like Jesus. Did you get that? I know some guys who live by the principles of utmost integrity. Let me go there for a second. This may sound pretentious and ostentatious, but some men have good hearts. I often feel that good men are underrated and if women invest more into a man's potential and focus less on his appearance or his wallet, then they may discover there's enough Jesus in a man for them.

What would be a realistic expectation of Jesus if he had been born in 1960 as opposed to 2,000 years ago? How would he handle the influence of modern-day thinking, the influences of technology, cultural differences or politics? Would he be inclined to think like one of us? After all, we are challenged with some of the same problems today as they were challenged with when Jesus was born: greed, corruption, distrust, food shortage, fuel shortage, overpopulation in some cities, and war. He would observe the same crimes, dishonor and deceit, just in different clothing. As a man is made to conform to his environment, would Jesus be tempted to perhaps be more human-like? I am sure Jesus would be surprised to find that although a many people still live off fish, an even larger number are overweight in America from having an abundance of food. He would find that people are no longer enslaved as punishment for their crimes or as a way to harvest the land and build the nation.

I would like to believe there is a Jesus out there for every woman. She will have to trust her own faith that she will either meet him soon or has already met or married him. Well, wait a minute, maybe Jesus isn't trying to get married at this time – maybe He prefers to remain available, in order to help the needy people of the world who are not being served. As for any ladies out there today who aren't trying to share their Jesus for fear that He may use his loving powers on another woman, shame on you. Think about it for a second, a modern-day Jesus Christ, what an amazing gift He could be to a dying world!

When I was a kid, I saw John F. Kennedy, our 35th president, as the latter-day Jesus Christ. On the day he died, I remember for the first time in my life I felt uncontrollably sad for a man I never met. I just knew he had risked his life for the equal rights of black people and we all wanted him to live. Then there was Martin Luther King, Jr., marching into my life like a dream that I wanted to wake up and live. He had to be the latter-day Jesus Christ too, because he changed laws, and the lives of so many of my people, and of people all over the world. I really didn't think there would be another Jesus-like man after Dr. King in my life time. Then along came a governor of Arkansas, whom I first saw on television in the early 1990s when he won his first presidential debate during his race for the White House. Governor Bill Clinton. He stole my heart and gained my support. As president, he promoted women's causes, turned the economy around, and created more jobs. People were able to buy homes again, gas prices were at an all time low, and the quality of life was high. I remember saying, Thank you Jesus, I got a chance to see Jesus in him before he passed the torch to Barack Obama, a man who began his political work as a community organizer, helping downtrodden people in small, poor neighborhoods — just like Jesus. The one thing the wives of these great American men had in common was that they had to share their husbands with the world. Imagine a world without the influence of these great men, had their wives refused to share them with us?

Unfortunately, today there are far too many undercover latter-day conservatives trying not to sin, while in their own special way they are reaching out from within. If you want Jesus, you'll have to come to him just as you are, seek His face and turn from your wicked ways.

A common quest shared among the female gender is the desire for a good man. The Bible often describes Jesus as a good and upright man, perfect in all his ways. The true characteristics and qualities of a good man must first be defined, and can be expressed in various ways. Many women formulate their opinion of an upright man based upon the characteristics they have seen in their grandfather, father, other male relatives or male friends. But is this truly the best way to define such an all-important figure?

There is another area of concern that most women struggle with: a man's ability to love. A man's ability to love often determines the nature of good and healthy relationships. The Bible speaks of four different types of love. *Eros* is the kind of love is that erotic and sensual, the kind of love that a woman desires to fulfill her sexual needs and solidify her oneness with her man. *Storge* refers to familial love. This family love is very important for a woman, as she depends on the man to be the chief provider and protector of the family. If a man loves his family, he will do whatever it takes to satisfy all of their needs, even if it means putting his aside. *Phileo* refers to brotherly and sisterly love. God has stated, "To obtain eternal life, a man must love the Lord with all his heart and soul and love his neighbor as himself." This neighbor to whom God is referring is thought of as the man's brother or sister. Finally, the ultimate love that a woman seeks from a man is a*gape*. Agape love is unconditional. This love is the most desired by every woman. It says, "I love you in spite of ..." This love suggests that no matter what flaws you have, no matter what issues you struggle with, no matter what problems you may create, I will never stop loving you. The man who can live up to the challenges that all these loves may bring about is truly a good, upright, Jesus-like man.

The question now is, how does a woman respond to an upright and good man? What if Jesus was one of us? If Jesus, perfect in all ways, was a man permitted to marry a woman, what would be the woman's response to Jesus? Ladies, be careful how you judge a man, he could be Jesus in disguise. I am trying to tell you: He's here for you, if you will just open your eyes.

Bibliography

Baisden, M. (2003). *God's Gift to Women*. New York, NY: Simon & Schuster Adult Publishing Group.

Bushong, C. (1997). *The Seven Dumbest Relationship Mistakes Smart People Make*. New York, NY: The Ballantine Publishing Group.

Carter, S. & Sokol, J. (1988). *Men Who Can't Love*. New York, NY: Berkley Publishing Group.

DeGenova, M. K. (2008). *Intimate Relationships, Marriages, & Families, 7th Edition*. New York, NY: McGraw-Hill.

Forward, S. (1999). *When Your Lover Is a Liar*. New York, NY: HarperCollins Publishers.

Glasser, W. (2000). *Getting Together and Staying Together*. New York, NY: Harper Paperbacks.

Harper, H. (2009). *The Conversation*. New York, NY: The Penguin Group.

Harvey, S. (2009). *Act Like a Lady, Think Like a Man*. New York, NY: HarperCollins Publishers.

Hopson, D. S. & Hopson, D. P. (1995). *Friends, Lovers and Soul Mates: A Guide to Better Relationships Between Black Men and Women*. New York, NY: Fireside.

Keen, S. (1992). *Fire In The Belly: On Being A Man.* New York, NY: Bantam Books.

Leone, B. & Swisher, K. L. (1995). *Human Sexuality: Opposing Viewpoints.* Farmington Hills, MI: Greenhaven Press.

McGraw, P. (2005). *Love Smart.* New York, NY: Free Press.

Olson, D. & DeFrain, J. (2002). *Marriages and Families: Intimacy, Diversity and Strengths, 4th Edition.* Upper Saddle River, NJ: Prentice Hall.

Strong, B., Devault, C., & Cohen, T. F. (2004). *The Marriage and Family Experience: Intimate Relationships in a Changing Society, 9th Edition.* Florence, KY: Wadsworth Publishing.

Tannen, D. (2001). *You Just Don't Understand.* New York, NY: Quill.

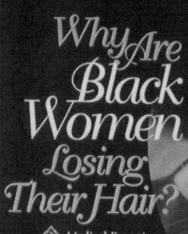

Why Are Black Women Losing Their Hair?

- ◈ *Medical Expertise*
- ◈ *Hair Loss Prevention*
- ◈ *Holistic Treatments*
- ◈ *Chemical Destruction*
- ◈ *Natural Hair Care*
- ◈ *Hair Growth Remedies*

The First Complete Guide To Healthy Hair

Barry Fletcher

Hair is Sexual

Are you sexually aware?
What makes a grown man stare?
It could be your hair!

by Barry Fletcher